Country Inn

COOKBOOK

Recipes from inns featured in "Country Inns and Back Roads"

Berkshire Traveller Press
Stockbridge, Massachusetts 01262

Selected Titles from the Berkshire Traveller Press:

COUNTRY INNS AND BACK ROADS
TREASURED RECIPES OF COUNTRY INNS
WAIT A MINUTE . . . I'LL GET YOU MY RECIPE
By Carol Bergeron
YOU CAN SAVE MONEY ON THAT MEAL
By Carol Bergeron

25 24 23 22 21 20 19 18 17

Illustrations by Janice Lindstrom

Library of Congress Catalog Card Number: 75-2520
The Berkshire Traveller (Norman Simpson)
Country Inn Cookbook, 2nd. ed.

© 1975 Berkshire Traveller Press, Stockbridge, Massachusetts
Revised Edition
ISBN #0-912944-18-8

A great deal of American innkeeping has its roots in Europe. However, unlike some Old World hostelries, the American Country Inn defies being prototyped. Each of the Inns in this volume is unique. It has a personality that is indigenous with its locale and its host.

These recipes, many of them treasured through generations of innkeeping, are frequently specialties of the inn. Standing in warm odoriferous kitchens, I jotted some down as the cook or chef busied himself with the whisks, ramkins, saucepans and kettles while reciting them from memory.

Although the American Country Inn is hard to find, I have discovered it isn't the extinct genus that it is sometimes portrayed.

True, I have turned off the turnpikes to small villages; wound my way up imposing mountains; and ventured on the side roads leading to the sea—but that's part of the game. It's part of the innate character of each inn—to be apart: to be special.

This book has been prepared with two equal thoughts. First: to add to your enjoyment at home. Second: to point out that traditional American hospitality may be a great deal closer than you imagine. Bon appetit and bon voyage!

The Berkshire Traveller

CONTENTS

SAUCY THINGS

Appetizers

ARTICHOKE & CRAB MEAT AU GRATIN
  Inn at Sawmill Farm; West Dover, Vermont
BROILED GRAPEFRUIT
  Chalet Suzanne; Lake Wales, Florida
CODFISH BALLS
  Barrows House; Dorset, Vermont
OYSTERS A LA GINO
  Robert Morris Inn; Oxford, Maryland

INN AT SAWMILL FARM
West Dover, Vermont

An exquisitely restored barn and farm outbuildings on a gurgling brook. In summer; morning sounds of birds, the sweet aroma of new mowed hay and the tranquility of grazing cows. In winter; skiing at Mt. Snow and Haystack.

ARTICHOKE & CRAB MEAT AU GRATIN

3 medium sized onions
¼ lb. butter
3 tbs. flour
2 cups table cream
1 lb. back fin crab meat (fresh)
2 tsp. Worcestershire sauce

Juice of ½ lemon
½ tsp. nutmeg
¼ cup Sherry wine
18 artichoke bottoms (canned)
½ cup Parmesan cheese
butter
dash paprika

Saute onions in butter taking care not to brown them, add flour and blend the two until smooth. Add cream gradually and stir constantly until thick. Add crab meat, Worcestershire sauce, lemon, nutmeg and sherry to taste.

Cover artichoke bottoms with crab meat mixture and top with Parmesan cheese, dab of butter and paprika. Brown under broiler and serve immediately to those who enjoy delicate crab meat.

CHALET SUZANNE
Lake Wales, Florida

The bridges, penthouses, steeples, cupolas, minarets, peaked-roofs, flat-roofs, castles, domes, doo-dads, treasures, junk, antiques and pagodas of Chalet Suzanne are incredible. This Broiled Grapefruit tops it all.

BROILED GRAPEFRUIT

PER SERVING:
½ grapefruit
½ tsp. sugar
1 tbs. butter

2 tbs. cinnamon-sugar mixture or enough to cover top well (1 part cinnamon to 4 parts sugar)
1 chicken liver, salted, peppered, floured and sauteed in butter

Have the grapefruit at room temperature so it will heat through when the top is browned. Cut around each section close to the membrane until the fruit is completely loosened from its shell. Cut a hole in the center of the grapefruit half and fill with butter. Sprinkle with sugar, then with cinnamon-sugar mixture. Broil 4 inches from heat for 8 to 10 minutes, or until top is browned and bubbling. At the end of broiling time, place the sauteed chicken liver in the center.

This makes a most unusual appetizer, and without the chicken liver, it can also be served for dessert. This is an original recipe of Chalet Suzanne. And when served at the Chalet, it is just a little better since the fruit is always freshly picked from their own citrus groves.

12

BARROWS HOUSE
Dorset, Vermont

Marilyn and Charlie Schubert each offer distinct contributions to making this beautiful village inn a most enjoyable experience. Charlie is a man of unfathomable energy and extremely good humor. Marilyn, a former airline stewardess, has these qualities in abundance plus an ability to organize.

NEW ENGLAND CODFISH BALLS

1 cup mashed potatoes	1 tbs. fresh dill, finely chopped or
1 lb. boneless salt codfish	2 tsp. dried dill weed
5-6 anchovy fillets, drained,	½ tsp. sage
washed, dried and	½ tsp. salt
finely chopped	⅛ tsp. cayenne pepper
2 egg yolks	1 cup flour
1 tbs. onion, finely grated	6 tbs. butter
1 tbs. butter, softened	2 tbs. vegetable oil

Soak codfish in water for 24 hours, changing the water several times. Poach the fish in enough water to cover until it flakes easily with a fork, 10 minutes. Drain. Combine codfish flakes, anchovies, mashed potatoes and beat vigorously with a large spoon until they are thoroughly blended and the mixture is smooth. Beat in egg yolks, one at a time, then add onion, butter, dill, sage, salt and cayenne pepper. If the mixture is not solid enough to hold its shape when formed into balls, beat in up to 3 tbs. bread crumbs. For easier handling, chill the mixture for at least an hour. Shape into small balls and roll them in flour. Heat the butter and oil in a heavy frying pan until sizzling and fry the codfish balls over high heat until crisp and deep brown. Serves 4 as a main course or 8 as an appetizer.
Once floured and shaped into balls, they can be frozen and brought out whenever needed. They make a fine hors d'oeuvres with or without a sauce.

ROBERT MORRIS INN
Oxford, Maryland

Best reached by the oldest (and probably smallest) car ferry in the country. Handsome early 18th century home with original beams, panels, floors and fireplaces. In the midst of unspoiled Chesapeake Bay waterways and countryside.

OYSTERS ALA GINO

24 oysters, shucked (in shell)
1 can lump crab meat (salt and pepper to taste)
½ pt. Newburg sauce
3 strips cooked bacon, chopped
¼ tsp. Accent

Dash Worcestershire sauce
½ cup sherry wine
1 lb. coarse ground bread crumbs
4 tbs. paprika
6 strips raw bacon, cut in squares
¼ tsp. garlic powder

Place shucked oysters on baking tray. Mix Newburg sauce, chopped bacon, garlic powder, Worcestershire sauce, Accent and wine; pour over crab meat. Mix lightly, fill oysters, mix butter with bread crumbs and paprika, sprinkle over oysters. Place a square of bacon on each oyster. Bake 10 minutes at 300 degrees. Serves 4 to 6.

Soups

WESTPORT CLAM CHOWDER
The Squire Tarbox House; Westport, Maine
CHILLED CUCUMBER SOUP
Colby Hill Inn; Henniker, New Hampshire
CREAM CHEESE SOUP
Blueberry Hill Farm; Goshen, Vermont
CREAM OF EGGPLANT SOUP
Morgan House; Lee, Massachusetts
EGG AND LEMON SOUP
The Claremont; Southwest Harbor, Maine
LOBSTER STEW
The Black Point Inn; Prouts Neck, Maine
PEANUT BUTTER SOUP
The Old Club; Alexandria, Virginia
STEAK SOUP
The Lyme Inn; Lyme, New Hampshire
ZUCCHINI SOUP
The Chester Inn; Chester, Vermont

SQUIRE TARBOX HOUSE
Westport, Maine

I love to sit in the kitchen at this Maine coast country inn and talk with Eleanor Smith and her sister, Mary Wright. This Westport clam chowder is a good example of some excellent New England home cooking.

WESTPORT CLAM CHOWDER

¼ lb. salt pork
2 medium onions, diced
3 medium Maine potatoes, diced
1½ cups water
1 pint fresh clams or 2 cans minced clams
2 cups rich milk or 1 can evaporated and 1 cup whole milk
    salt and pepper to taste
2 tbs. butter

Try out the salt pork; remove and reserve the crisp bits of pork. Add onions and saute until clear but not brown. Add the potatoes and water and simmer until the potatoes are tender. Add the clams and then the milk; heat to boiling point, but do not boil. Season to taste. Add butter and crisp bits of pork. Serve hot with crackers.

For something a little different, I've used this same recipe to make a delicious fish chowder. Just substitute 2 cups of poached fish and 1½ cups of fish broth for the clams and water.

COLBY HILL INN
Henniker, New Hampshire

Bettie Gilbert is both innkeeper and cook at this serene white clapboard inn. The first time I met her she was making this chilled cucumber soup.

CHILLED CUCUMBER SOUP

1¼ cups cream of chicken soup (undiluted)
½ cup milk
1 cucumber, peeled and sliced
8 oz. sour cream
    dash of curry powder
    dash of minced onion
    salt and pepper to taste

Combine all ingredients in a blender and blend well. Chill until ready to serve. Serve in chilled cups, garnished with chopped chives.

BLUEBERRY HILL INN
Goshen, Vermont

Blueberry Hill, high in the Vermont mountains between Brandon and Ripton, is set in glorious isolation on a back road next to the Green Mountain National Forest where there are approximately 45 miles of cross country ski trails. Guests at this inn sit around the long table and enjoy family-style meals.

CREAM CHEESE SOUP

4 stalks celery	2 cups beer or water
8 large leeks, bottoms	16 oz. cream cheese
6 tbs. flour	2 cups sour cream
5 cups chicken broth	Sprinkling of chopped green herbs
	(chives, dill, parsley)

Chop the celery and leeks, and saute in butter. Do not brown. Blend in flour, broth and beer and simmer for 10 minutes. Cream together the cream cheese and sour cream. Either blend the hot soup in a blender or run it through a sieve; then add to the cream cheese mixture. Reheat but do not boil, and sprinkle with fresh, chopped herbs. Serves 8.

MORGAN HOUSE
Lee, Massachusetts

A hundred years ago the Morgan House was a popular lodging house for traveling theatrical companies. Today, you can read their scroll-embellished names on the old register sheets, which are now used to paper the lobby.

CREAM OF EGGPLANT SOUP

1/3 cup onion, minced	2 cups milk
1/3 cup celery, minced	2 cups light cream
1 eggplant, peeled and diced	salt and pepper to taste
6 tbs. butter	pinch of marjoram
6 tbs. flour	1/3 cup Chablis wine
2 cups chicken stock	

Saute onion, celery and eggplant in butter until tender. Stir in flour, then add chicken stock gradually. Let this come to a boil. Add heated milk and cream; do not boil. Add seasonings and wine. Serves 6.

THE CLAREMONT INN
Southwest Harbor, Maine

The Claremont overlooks Somes Sound on the Mt. Desert Island in Maine. The first time I heard about this egg and lemon soup I had some misgivings, but after the first hesitant sip I became a devotee. Perhaps you will too.

EGG AND LEMON SOUP

6 cups chicken stock
3 eggs

¼ cup fresh lemon juice
1 lemon, sliced

Salt the chicken stock to taste and bring to a boil. Beat eggs until pale yellow, then beat in lemon juice. Remove the stock from the heat and slowly add two cups of stock to the egg mixture, whisking vigorously. Pour this mixture into the remaining stock; whisk until slightly thickened. Cool to room temperature, then refrigerate. Serve chilled and garnished with lemon slices.

THE BLACK POINT INN
Prouts Neck, Maine

Prouts Neck near Portland, has bay and ocean waters, white sand beaches, rugged cliffs, gracious homes, memories of Winslow Homer, and the intimate passions of the sea. It also has The Black Point Inn. This is the inn of which I have said: "She's like a beautiful woman—poised, gracious, well dressed, interesting and above all interested."

LOBSTER STEW

1 lb. lobster meat
½ cup butter
pinch nutmeg
1 tsp. paprika
⅛ cup Worcestershire sauce
1 oz. sherry wine
1 qt. light cream
1 qt. regular milk
salt and pepper

Melt butter in heavy pot, add paprika, nutmeg and lobster meat. Cook slowly for half hour. Heat milk and cream (do not boil). Add to lobster meat. Season to taste. Add white wine just before serving. 10 servings.

THE OLD CLUB
Alexandria, Virginia

Peanut Butter Soup is just one of the typically Southern dishes which first attracted me to the Old Club. This old colonial building in Alexandria, Virginia, just a few minutes from downtown Washington, D.C., was once George Washington's club.

PEANUT BUTTER SOUP

1 qt. rich chicken stock	3 oz. butter
3 oz. minced onions	1 tbs. flour
3 oz. minced celery	1 cup Half & Half (milk & cream)
8 oz. peanut butter	1 tsp. salt
	¼ tsp. pepper

Simmer chicken stock, onions and celery together for 45-60 minutes. Strain out onion and celery and discard. Stir in peanut butter until dissolved. Mix flour with Half and Half, add together with remaining ingredients, simmer all together 15 minutes. Garnish with ½ teaspoon bacon crumbs or minced country ham. Serves 8-10.

THE LYME INN
Lyme, New Hampshire

Lyme, with its sizeable boat-shaped village green, boasts a most interesting church and an equally interesting inn of its very own. It has quaint old-fashioned rooms, antique furnishings and hearty New England food.

STEAK SOUP

1/2 lb. margarine	1 pkg. corn, frozen
1 cup flour	1/3 cup beef stock base
2 qts. boiling water	1/2 cup dry vermouth
2 large carrots, diced	2 lbs. ground beef, browned
1 large onion, diced	pepper
2 large stalks celery and leaves, diced	parsley, chopped
1 16 oz. can tomatoes	salt

Melt margarine, add flour and cook for a few minutes. Add boiling water and stir until smooth. Add remaining ingredients and simmer for 4 hours.

THE CHESTER INN
Chester, Vermont

Young urban expatriates Jim and Audrey Patterson, have put new vigor into this central Vermont village inn so well situated for summer and winter diversions. The recipe below is one of several for which Audrey, young and pretty though she may be, is already well known.

ZUCCHINI SOUP

4 cups sliced zucchini (with skin on)
1½ quarts chicken stock or canned chicken broth
½ cup chopped onion
1 cup fresh cream
2 tbs. butter
1 tsp. basil
fresh or dried chives

In large saucepan saute onion in butter for 2-3 minutes. Add zucchini, basil and chicken stock. Simmer 30 minutes until zucchini is very tender. Remove from heat. Put through food mill. Add cream. Season to taste. Serve hot or cold. (If serving hot reheat to simmer only without boiling.) Garnish with fresh chopped chives. Serves 8.

Meats

BEEF BOURGUIGNON
New London Inn; New London, New Hampshire
BEEF LUAU
The Homestead Inn; Greenwich, Connecticut
RAGOUT DE BOULETTES
Hovey Manor; North Hatley, Quebec
LOS CABALLEROS MEXICAN TACO
Rancho de los Caballeros; Wickenburg, Arizona
STEAK AND KIDNEY PIE
Stagecoach Hill; Sheffield, Massachusetts
VEAL MARSALA
Red Lion Inn; Stockbridge, Massachusetts
FROG'S LEGS SAUTEED IN CHABLIS WINE
The Botsford Inn; Farmington, Michigan
CAPTAIN WHIDBEY HAM AND MUSHROOM CASSEROLE
The Captain Whidbey; Coupeville, Washington
KENTUCKY COUNTRY HAM
Inn at Pleasant Hill; Shakertown, Kentucky
MONTE CRISTO SANDWICH
Middlebury Inn; Middlebury, Vermont
PORK LOIN STUFFED WITH PRUNES AND APPLES
The Normandy Inn; Louisville, Kentucky

SAUTEED PORK CHOPS GLEN IRIS
Glen Iris Inn; Castile, New York
SEKELEY GULYAS
The Farmhouse; Port Townsend, Washington
SWEET AND SOUR PORK RICE O'BRIEN
Beekman Arms; Rhinebeck, New York

NEW LONDON INN
New London, New Hampshire

We left Boston at 6 and drove through the twilight in those rapturous New Hampshire hills, sighting the lights and colonial outlines of the New London Inn at 8. The fireplace was crackling and the aroma from the kitchen bespoke great promise. The rooms were bright and cheerful and the air was clean and sweet. Our New London weekend had started!

NEW LONDON INN BEEF BOURGUIGNON

2 tbs. oleo or vegetable oil	¼ tsp. marjoram
5 medium onions, cut up	¼ tsp. thyme
½ lb. mushrooms	⅛ tsp. pepper
2 lbs. boneless chuck beef,	1½ tbs. flour
cut into 1 inch cubes	¾ cup beef broth
1 tsp. salt	1½ cups burgundy

Melt oleo and add onions and mushrooms. Cook and stir until the onions are tender. Remove vegetables and drain off the liquid. Brown the beef cubes. Mix together the spices and flour and sprinkle over browned beef. Mix well, then add broth and simmer 1½ to 2 hours. Stir in burgundy and add onions and mushrooms. Serve over rice or noodles.

THE HOMESTEAD INN
Greenwich, Connecticut

The Homestead is a country inn with large comfortable rooms, handsome period furniture, lots of trees, grass, birds, butterflies, peace and quiet and well-favored food. The recipe below is a good example. Best of all, it's in Greenwich. Connecticut, just 45 minutes from New York City.

BEEF LUAU

3 to 4 lbs. shortribs
1 tsp. salt
1 can pineapple bits
½ cup catsup
¼ cup water

½ cup onion, minced
¼ cup green pepper, chopped
3 tbs. brown sugar
½ tsp. dry mustard
½ tsp. salt

Sprinkle the meat with salt and brown in a Dutch oven or heavy skillet. Pour off drippings, cover and cook slowly for 1½ hours. Pour off drippings again. Combine remaining ingredients and add to the shortribs. Cover and cook another 20 minutes. This dish smelled extravagant and tasted even better. When I got home and tried the recipe myself, I was really surprised at how easy it was to make and, best of all, so inexpensive!

HOVEY MANOR
North Hatley, Quebec

Hovey Manor is the place where they speak three languages: English, French and hospitality. It is located on the shores of Lake Massawippi about an hour from Montreal to the north and the U. S. border to the south.

RAGOUT DE BOULETTES
(French Canadian Meatball Stew)

3 lbs. ground beef
1 tbs. salt
1 tbs. pepper
cinnamon to taste
whole cloves to taste
8-10 small potatoes, sliced
8-10 small whole carrots
beef bouillon
thyme to taste

Mix half of the spices with the ground beef and form into balls. Roll the meatballs in flour and brown in a frying pan. Partially cook the vegetables and add to the frying pan. Make a brown sauce or add beef bouillon. Add thyme and the remaining spices. Cook until vegetables are tender and sauce thick.

RANCHO DE LOS CABALLEROS
Wickenburg, Arizona

What a change for a New Englander—a winter vacation at a luxury guest ranch in the high desert country. Swimming, tennis, hunting and of course, riding. Dress is casual and children have their own activities.

LOS CABALLEROS MEXICAN TACO

24 corn tortillas
2 lbs. hamburger
3 large onions, chopped fine
1 tsp. salt
1 tsp. whole Mexican oregano

3 cups green chili salsa
celery salt and pepper to taste
1 cup flour
grated cheese
shredded lettuce and diced tomatoes

Cook tortillas in deep fat until crisp. Combine onions, hamburger, salt, oregano, salsa, celery salt and pepper, and cook until brown. Add 1 cup flour and blend.

Put about 3 oz. of this taco meat mixture in corn tortilla. Sprinkle with grated cheese on top and place in 375 degrees oven for 5 min. Remove and top with shredded lettuce and diced tomato. Serve with Mexican hot sauce.

STAGECOACH HILL
Sheffield, Massachusetts

A bit of fair Albion in the Berkshires. This former stage stop is a red brick colonial with a British innkeeper and a saucy air that is quite infectious.

STEAK AND KIDNEY PIE

1 lb. choice top round
1 good size lamb kidney
1 onion

1 pint beef stock
1 bay leaf
1 pie pastry

Chop the onion fine, saute it in butter, and season with salt, pepper, and bay leaf. Add the top round diced into half inch cubes; then saute meat until brown. Add the beefstock and simmer slowly until tender, approximately one hour. Add the kidney which has been peeled, with the center fat removed, and diced. Allow the mixture to cook a little longer—about 10 minutes. Let it cool, place in pie pan, cover with a rich pastry crust, and bake until done. This is best when served by a pretty country lass with light 'o love in her eye, and a song on her lips. Something by the Beatles, no doubt.

RED LION INN
Stockbridge, Massachusetts

Stockbridge is the Berkshires viewed through towering elms. It is broad lawns, church steeples, childrens' chimes, nearby meadows and meandering streams. It is also the Red Lion Inn, first built in 1773 and now happily open year 'round. We frequently dine at the new Widow Bingham's Tavern, and the entrée below is particularly savory.

VEAL MARSALA

PER SERVING:

6 veal medallions (thin slices cut in 1½ inch squares)
flour for dredging
2 tbs. butter
salt and pepper to taste

2 tbs. onions, chopped fine
handful of mushrooms, sliced
pinch of parsley
½ cup Marsala wine
½ cup beef stock

Coat the veal medallions with flour. Add veal, with butter, salt and pepper and onions, to a pan and brown on both sides. Pour off excess butter. Add mushrooms, parsley and Marsala; flame the Marsala until it burns completely off. Add beef stock and cook until thickened.

THE BOTSFORD INN
Farmington Hills, Michigan

The Botsford is a Michigan anachronism...a small sheltered corner that appears to be untouched by the 20th Century. Not quite untouched, for although it is Michigan's oldest inn and dates to 1836, with antiques and memorabilia of gentler times, it has the most modern conveniences, and is quite close-at-hand to downtown Detroit.

FROGS' LEGS SAUTEED IN CHABLIS WINE

pinch white pepper
pinch salt
1 cup flour
2 eggs

1 cup milk
6-8 medium frogs legs
4 tbs. butter
1 oz. Chablis wine
paprika

Mix salt, pepper, flour in pan. Mix eggs with milk. Place frogs' legs in egg and milk mixture for one minute, then drop into flour mixture. Heat butter in heavy skillet and drop frogs' legs into hot butter. Brown on both sides, sprinkle with paprika and add Chablis. Cover with foil and place in 350 degree oven for 10 minutes. Serve on toast. To me the most difficult thing about serving frogs' legs has to be catching the frogs. I'm sorry that John Anhut didn't include instructions for stalking these elusive creatures.

THE CAPTAIN WHIDBEY INN
Coupeville, Washington

How about a true New England inn run by an honest-to-goodness native of Nantucket Island, Massachusetts — but located on an island just a ferry ride away from Seattle! I enjoy preparing this ham and mushroom casserole.

CAPTAIN WHIDBEY HAM AND MUSHROOM CASSEROLE

3 cups bread crumbs
12 hard-boiled eggs, sliced
1 lb. fresh mushrooms, whole
3 cups ham, cut in ½'' cubes
1 lb. butter, divided

1 qt. milk
½ cup sherry
1 cup flour
1 tsp. MSG
½ tsp. white pepper
salt to taste

Toast bread crumbs in ½ lb. butter until golden. Make a roux of ½ lb. melted butter and flour. Add milk and sherry all at once and stir until thickened. Add seasonings to taste. In a 12x8x4 inch baking dish, layer the bread crumbs, eggs, mushrooms, ham and sherry sauce, ending with a layer of bread crumbs over all. Bake in a 350 degree oven for 45 minutes or until heated through.

INN AT PLEASANT HILL
Shakertown, Kentucky

Pleasant Hill is a Shaker restoration near Beaumont including some magnificent "Shaker Georgian" buildings in native lime-stone, red brick and occasional yellow clapboard. As far as I know, it is the only restored historic village in the country where visitors may spend the night in the original buildings.

KENTUCKY COUNTRY HAM

1 country ham	1 cup brown sugar
½ cup whole cloves	1 cup corn meal
1 cup brown sugar	1 tbs. ground cloves
1 cup vinegar	1 tsp. cinnamon

Scrub ham and soak in water overnight. Sprinkle some of the cloves on bottom of a roaster and some on top of the ham. Add about one inch of water. Put 1 cup of brown sugar and vinegar around ham. Cook for 1 hour in a 375 degree oven. Then turn temperature down to 275 degrees and cook 20 minutes per pound. Remove from roaster. Bone if desired and trim if necessary. Mix together 1 cup of brown sugar, corn meal, ground cloves and cinnamon. Sprinkle the ham with this mixture and brown in a 375 degree oven.

MIDDLEBURY INN
Middlebury, Vermont

I like to visit the Middlebury Inn during the football season because it is such great fun to see this bustling Vermont village overflowing with eager collegians. Some of their youthful appetites are assuaged with this distinctly unique Middlebury Inn specialty.

MONTE CRISTO SANDWICH

2 slices day-old bread	2 slices Swiss cheese
1 egg, well beaten	sliced ham

Dip one side of bread into well-beaten egg, then brown on a greased grill or in a skillet. Assemble the sandwich, cooked side in; place sliced ham between the cheese slices. Secure with a toothpick. Dip both outsides of the sandwich in the egg and grill. For interesting variations of this sandwich, try making it with sliced turkey or corned beef in place of the ham.

THE NORMANDY INN
Louisville, Kentucky

Just looking at the title and ingredients of this recipe makes me hungry. The Normandy is a very impressive restaurant on the waterfront of Louisville, Kentucky. Its restored building has already become a well-known landmark.

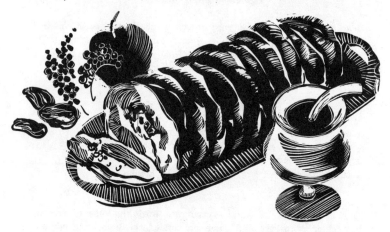

PORK LOIN STUFFED WITH PRUNES AND APPLES

4-5 lb. boneless pork loin	¾ cup heavy cream
1 cup pitted prunes, chopped coarsely	1 tbs. currant jelly
1 cup fresh apples cut into 1'' cubes	¼ cup currants
1 cup dry white wine	

Make a slit the length of the loin within ½ inch of the end and to within 1 inch of the other side. Into this pocket, place the prepared pitted prunes and the raw apples. Tie the loin with twine at two inch intervals.

Preheat oven to 350. Brown loin in a roasting pan which, with occasional turning, should take about 20 minutes. Remove grease from pan and add 1 cup dry white wine, and stir in ¾ cup heavy cream, currant jelly and currants. Return to oven, cover and cook for 1½ hours.

GLEN IRIS INN
Castile, New York

The Glen Iris Inn is located in the southern end of beautiful Letchworth State Park in the western part of New York State. It overlooks the gorgeous falls of the Genesee River, and is surrounded by attractive gardens and broad lawns.

SAUTEED PORK CHOPS GLEN IRIS

2 tbs. butter	3 cups fresh mushrooms, sliced
8 4-5 oz. pork chops, center cut	4 tomatoes cut in wedges
2 tbs. butter	salt and pepper to taste
1 large onion, coarsely sliced	1 clove garlic, minced

Saute pork chops in butter over medium heat 4 or 5 minutes. Arrange in baking pan and put in 400 degree oven until done.

In saute pan add more butter, saute onion 2 or 3 minutes. Add mushrooms and saute 2 more minutes, then add tomatoes and garlic. Cook until tomatoes are done but still firm.

Remove pork chops from oven and place on hot serving platter and spread sauteed ingredients evenly over pork chops.

THE FARM HOUSE
Port Townsend, Washington

James Beard refers to the Farm House as his "first restaurant." It may well be that John Ashby Conway, who is both innkeeper and chef is one of the best gourmet cooks in the country. This Sekeley Gulyas is typical of some of the unusual main dishes that are served at this restaurant located on the shores of Juan de Fuca. If you are going to visit be sure to phone Dorothy Conway for directions and reservations.

SEKELEY GULYAS FARMHOUSE

2½ lbs. pork shoulder,
   cut into 1½'' cubes
2 large onions, sliced thin
4 tbs. Hungarian sweet paprika
2 small cans tomato paste
1 cup chicken stock

2½ lbs. sauerkraut
2 cloves garlic, crushed
1 tbs. caraway seed, moistened
   and pounded in a mortar
1 cup sour cream

Dredge the pork cubes in flour and brown in lard or soy oil. Reserve the rendered fat. Saute onions in the pork fat until transparent. Blend in paprika, then tomato paste. Add enough chicken stock to make a thick stew. Add sauerkraut, garlic, caraway seeds and pork cubes. If necessary add more chicken stock. Allow it to blend and cook in a 350 degree oven for at least one hour.

Half an hour before serving, add sour cream mixed with a little flour. This will thicken and flavor the gulyas. Return it to the oven for another 30 minutes, but do not allow to boil. Serve with homemade spaetzle and sweet and sour red cabbage. Serves 4-6.

If half of the sauerkraut is rinsed and drained in cold water before cooking, it will lower the acidity. Taste for salt before serving. One teaspoon Juniper Berries adds a nice flavor to the Gulyas.

BEEKMAN ARMS
Rhinebeck, New York

Established in 1701 and reputed to be America's oldest inn, the Beekman Arms has seen visits from Jefferson, Burr, Washington, Hamilton and two Roosevelts. Today its colonial atmosphere, antiques and hearty good food make it an adventure in early American hospitality.

SWEET AND SOUR PORK RICE O'BRIEN

2½ lbs. pork, one inch cubes
1½ cups flour
3 large green peppers, sliced
1 large can pineapple chunks or
   one cut up fresh pineapple
1 cup brown sugar
1 tsp. salt

¼ cup diced green peppers
½ cup white vinegar
½ cup dark molasses
5 cups peeled tomatoes
1 tbs. cornstarch
½ tsp. pepper
¼ cup diced red peppers

Brown pork lightly in the flour. Add liquid ingredients including tomatoes and bring to boil. Add dry ingredients and cook until pork is tender. Now add cornstarch for thickening if necessary. Serve in casserole, accompanied with buttered rice and diced red and green peppers. 8 servings.

Poultry

BREAST DE POULET BRAZILIAN COURT
  Brazilian Court Hotel; Palm Beach, Florida
BUTTERMILK PECAN CHICKEN
  The Patchwork Quilt; Middlebury, Indiana
CHICKEN CON QUESO
  Sagebrush Inn; Taos, New Mexico
CHICKEN SAUTE BENBOW
  Benbow Inn; Garberville, California
GRILLED CHICKEN DIABLE
  Swiss Hutte; Hillsdale, New York
STAFFORD'S CHICKEN IN HERB SAUCE
  Stafford's Bay View Inn; Petoskey, Michigan
ESCALLOPED TURKEY
  The Wells Inn; Sistersville, West Virginia
SUDBURY ROCK CORNISH HENS
  Sudbury Inn; Bethel, Maine

THE BRAZILIAN COURT
Palm Beach, Florida

The Brazilian Court has its yearly group of very devoted enthusiasts. I love evening meals here under the blue sky and gaily colored lights.

BREAST DE POULET BRAZILIAN COURT

1 chicken (3 lbs.)
butter
chicken stock

dry sauterne
1 cup white grapes
½ cup white wine

Bone the breast and second joints of the chicken and remove the skin. Poach in sauterne for 10 minutes, making a rich sauce from butter and chicken stock. Pour sauce over chicken in a covered skillet and simmer for 15 minutes. Add grapes and white wine. Serve on a bed of rice. Serves 4-5.

PATCHWORK QUILT
Middlebury, Indiana

This is the famous prize winning recipe from Milton and Arletta Lovejoy's Patchwork Quilt in Middlebury, Indiana. The cooking is done by the ladies of the neighborhood, many with their own specialities, but this recipe is Arletta's alone. Middlebury is in the vicinity of Elkhart and South Bend, on the route between Cleveland and Chicago.

BUTTERMILK PECAN CHICKEN

2 broiler-frying chickens,
    cut in serving pieces
½ cup butter or margarine
1 cup buttermilk
1 egg, slightly beaten
1 cup flour

1 cup pecans, ground
1 tbs. paprika
1 tbs. salt
⅛ tsp. pepper
¼ cup sesame seeds
¼ cup pecan halves

Melt butter in large shallow dish, 13x9x2 inch size. Mix buttermilk with egg in shallow dish. Mix flour, ground pecans, paprika, salt, pepper and sesame seeds in another. Dip chicken in buttermilk mixture, then flour mixture. Place skin side down in melted butter in baking dish, then turn pieces to coat chicken and place skin side up. Place pecan halves around chicken and bake in moderate oven for 1¾ hours or until tender and golden-brown. Garnish with parsley and cherry tomatoes. Serves 8.

SAGEBRUSH INN
Taos, New Mexico

The building and lodging rooms of this inn are all built of adobe brick. The entire feeling — the rugs, wall hangings, lamps, doors and door latches — is unquestionably New Mexican, along with the food. From the distinctly southwestern dishes that are always on the menu, I chose this unusually tasty chicken — it will taste best when in full view of Taos mountain!

CHICKEN CON QUESO

1 fryer chicken, cut in pieces
1 tbs. flour
1 tsp. salt
¼ tsp. pepper
2 green onions, chopped
2 cans cheddar cheese soup
1 cup water
1 small can evaporated milk
2 tsp. salt
½ clove garlic, chopped
dash of cumin
1 small tomato, chopped
1 can green chili, chopped
1 cup corn chips, roughly crumbled

Coat chicken with seasoned flour. Place skin side down in a baking pan, with melted shortening covering the bottom of the pan. Bake 1 hour in a 425 degree oven. Pour off the fat and turn chicken. Saute the green onions in chicken drippings. Add the remaining ingredients except corn chips and bring to a boil, stirring often. Spoon hot queso sauce over the chicken and bake in a 375 degree oven for 45 minutes or until tender. Baste with the sauce while baking. During the last 10 minutes of baking, sprinkle with crumbled corn chips. If desired, the chicken may be covered during the last 45 minutes. Serves 4.

BENBOW INN
Garberville, California

Garberville, California is located in the heart of the magnificent Redwood country on Route 101 in northern California. It is truly impossible to describe these tremendous, magnificent living giants. Benbow looks out over the bend of the Eel River. After a day in the forest it's good to come back to a hearty dinner such as this house specialty.

CHICKEN SAUTE BENBOW

1 spring chicken,
    cut into six pieces
2 oz. drawn butter
⅛ tsp. oregano
⅛ tsp. sweet basil
dash of garlic salt
dash of fresh ground pepper

½ cup dry sherry
¾ cup chicken broth
1 tsp. green peppers, diced
2 tsp. green onions, finely cut
½ cup fresh mushrooms, sliced
flour for dredging chicken

Dredge chicken in flour and saute in drawn butter over medium heat until browned on both sides. Pour off drawn butter and return pan to high heat, adding spices and vegetables immediately. Add sherry and bring to a boil (or flame the sherry.) Hold over high heat for one minute, then reduce to medium heat and simmer 15 minutes on each side or until the liquid has been reduced by one third. Serve with rice pilaf.

SWISS HUTTE
Hillsdale, New York

A nostalgic remembrance of a sequestered Swiss valley in the Berkshires, featuring a spectacular view of Catamount ski area both winter and summer. The menu is European, the atmosphere is Alpine.

GRILLED CHICKEN DIABLE

2½ lb. broiling chicken
2 tbs. Dijon mustard
4 tbs. bread crumbs
¼ cup melted butter

dash thyme
dash tarragon
salt and pepper

Split chicken and place on broiler rack. Season with salt, pepper, thyme and tarragon. Brush with melted butter and broil 15 minutes on each side, constantly basting the chicken with butter. Remove from broiling rack, pour drippings from chicken into a bowl. Beat the Dijon mustard into the drippings with a wire whip. Spread this mixture over chicken. Press bread crumbs over all, and place in 400 degree oven until golden brown. This dish should be garnished with broiled tomatoes, bacon strips and shoestring potatoes.

STAFFORD'S BAY VIEW INN
Petoskey, Michigan

The Bay View section of Petoskey, on the northeast shores of Lake Michigan, has remained unchanged since the last century. The Stafford Inn maintains the ambiance of the Victorian age, but with many decidedly modern touches.

STAFFORD'S CHICKEN IN HERB SAUCE

3 frying chickens (halved, or quartered)
salt
pepper
paprika
margarine, melted

SAUCE:

2 cups light cream or whole milk
2 10½ oz. cans cream of mushroom soup (a good brand will not separate)
½ cup strong chicken broth (2 boullion cubes per ½ cup hot water)

½ medium onion, minced
¼ cup dry, white wine
½ tsp. each rosemary, thyme, marjoram, basil
pinch of sage

Prepare your chicken using one of the following methods:

Dip in flour seasoned with salt, pepper and paprika and pan fry until golden brown and almost done; or place chicken in greased shallow pan, sprinkle with salt, pepper, paprika and melted margarine. Bake until golden brown and almost done.

Place prepared chicken in shallow baking pan or dish. Mix all ingredients of sauce together except herbs. Sprinkle herbs on chicken. Pour sauce over chicken, cover and bake in 325 degree oven for 45 minutes. Do not over-bake as sauce will separate if it simmers too long. Remove cover last 15 minutes to allow chicken to brown. Serve over favorite rice pilaf.

THE WELLS INN
Sistersville, West Virginia

Sistersville and the Wells Inn are a flashback to the days of 19th century opulence. It is a turn-of-the-century oil boom town and the Wells Inn has set a model for the restoration and preservation of Victorian decor. It is south of Wheeling on the Ohio River where crossing is made on a very picturesque ferry.

ESCALLOPED TURKEY

6 cups unseasoned croutons	¼ tsp. sweet basil
2 medium onions, sliced	¼ cup dry parsley
¾ tsp. sage	2 cups celery, finely chopped
2 tsp. salt	with leaves
½ tsp. pepper	6 cups hot turkey broth
1 tsp. thyme	6 cups boned turkey

Combine the first nine ingredients. Pour the boiling broth over the mixture, enough to make the croutons soft but not mushy. Stir, then cover and allow to steep for 15 minutes. Mix again to be sure croutons are moist. In alternating layers, put the dressing and small pieces of boned turkey in a baking pan. Allow for a layer of dressing on the bottom and top of the pan. Bake at 300 degrees for 30 minutes. Serve topped with turkey gravy.

SUDBURY INN
Bethel, Maine

The Sudbury Inn in Bethel, Maine (a town with 2 country inns) has created a way of cooking these that deserves all our attention. I have never had a failure with this recipe.

SUDBURY ROCK CORNISH HENS

2 Rock Cornish hens	¼ tsp. dried thyme, crushed
2 cups cheese crackers, crushed	dash of pepper
CHEESE MIXTURE:	
1/3 cup sour cream	1 tbs. dried onion flakes
2 tbs. blue cheese crumbled	1 clove garlic, minced
	salt to taste

Combine all of the ingredients for the cheese mixture and beat until smooth. Allow to stand at room temperature for 2 hours. Split hens lengthwise and remove the wing tips and end joints of the legs. Pat dry and dip the hens into the cheese mixture, then in a mixture of cracker crumbs, thyme and pepper. Place the coated hens on a lightly greased pan, skin side up. Bake in a 350 degree oven for 1 hour.

Seafood

BAKED STUFFED CAPE BLUEFISH
  Yankee Pedlar Inn; Holyoke, Massachusetts
CASCO BAY SURPRISE
  Homewood Inn; Yarmouth, Maine
CHEF GOELLER'S CREATION
  Inn at Rancho Santa Fe; Rancho Santa Fe, California
CRAB CAKES
  Maryland Inn; Annapolis, Maryland
CREOLE JAMBALAYA
  Lamothe House; New Orleans, Louisiana
DEEP DISH CLAM PIE
  American Hotel; Freehold, New Jersey
LOBSTER PROVENCALE AU WILD RICE
  Hotel Algonquin, New York, New York
FILLET OF FISH
  1740 House; Lumberville, Pennsylvania
PAN FRIED PICKEREL
  St. Clair Inn; St. Clair, Michigan
MARTHA'S VINEYARD SCALLOPED SCALLOPS
  Harborside Inn; Martha's Vineyard, Massachusetts
SCALLOPED OYSTERS
  The Red Inn; Provincetown, Massachusetts
SALMA-CADO
  Cold Spring Tavern; Santa Barbara, California

YANKEE PEDLAR INN
Holyoke, Massachusetts

This inn provides many travellers with their first taste of New England food and traditional New England hospitality. There are several different dining rooms, all decorated and furnished in the modes of earlier times. This baked stuffed bluefish is one of many hearty country items on the menu.

BAKED STUFFED CAPE BLUEFISH

16 oz. fillet
1 cup coarse fresh bread crumbs
1 clove garlic, chopped
½ tsp. black pepper, freshly ground

½ tsp. salt
1 oz. anchovies, chopped
1 tbs. parsley, chopped
olive oil

Mix bread crumbs with chopped garlic, black pepper, salt, anchovies and parsley. Add olive oil mixing constantly with fork until mixture is thoroughly moist. Spread mixture over top of fish and bake for about 20 minutes in 300 degree oven.

THE HOMEWOOD INN
Yarmouth, Maine

Fred, Colleen and Doris Webster always have the latchstring out for tired and hungry travelers. This inn is on the shores of Casco Bay.

CASCO BAY SURPRISE

2 cups fresh crabmeat, flaked
¼ cup mayonnaise
½ tsp. Worcestershire sauce
½ tsp. lemon juice
12 slices of bread, lightly toasted

1 cup sharp cheddar cheese, shredded
3 hard-boiled eggs, sliced
12 slices bacon, broiled
½ cup stuffed olives, chopped

Cut six slices of toast diagonally. Mix the first four ingredients and spread over all the toast. Arrange on a baking sheet with one whole toast, flanked by two halves. Sprinkle with cheese and broil until the cheese is melted. Arrange on a serving plate with one slice of bacon on either side of whole toast and egg slices down the middle. Sprinkle egg slices with chopped olives. Serve with pickles and chips. Makes 6 open faced sandwiches.
And for those of us who don't live on the shore and can't always get fresh crabmeat, tunafish makes a fine substitute!

INN AT RANCHO SANTA FE
Rancho Santa Fe

One of the traditions at this inn is that the innkeeper makes it a point to visit individually with every guest during their stay. The grounds are beautiful, dominated by lush eucalyptus and acacia trees.

CHEF GOELLER'S CREATION

½ lobster tail, diced
3 shrimp, split
3 oz. veal
3 oz. pork tenderloin,
salt, pepper, garlic, curry,
   paprika and MSG to taste
½ medium onion
½ bell pepper
1 jalapeno pepper
1 stalk celery

5 jumbo mushrooms, fresh
½ apple, peeled
1 handful seedless grapes
½ fresh mango
2 rings canned pineapple
¼ papaya, julienne sliced
1 tbs. mango chutney
4 oz. bottle ketchup
2 oz. bottle steak sauce
1 tsp. Worcestershire sauce

Cut vegetables, fruit and pork to size of french fries.

In one skillet saute the first four ingredients with seasonings to taste. In a second skillet saute the vegetables and fruits, with seasonings to taste. Add chutney, ketchup, steak sauce and Worcestershire sauce to the sauteed fruits and vegetables. Combine all of the ingredients together and serve over rice. And if that isn't unusual or flavorful enough, serve with a rice creole or pantsi long rice! Serves 4-5.

MARYLAND INN
Annapolis, Maryland

Every square foot of Annapolis is laden with three centuries of history and more is being made every day! At the Maryland Inn we dined in the Ordinary with admirals, legislators, foreign dignitaries and mid-shipmen and their "drags." Maryland Crab is one of the specialties and my mouth waters with anticipation when I see this recipe.

CRAB CAKES

2 lb. crabmeat
7 slices white bread
  diced, crusts removed
1/4 green pepper, chopped
1/8 cup parsley, chopped
2 eggs
10 tbs mayonnaise
1 2/3 tsp. dry mustard
1/2 tsp. salt
3 shakes Tabasco
1 1/2 shakes Worcestershire sauce
1 tbs. lemon juice

Beat eggs lightly and add mayonnaise, mustard, salt, Tabasco, Worcestershire sauce and lemon juice. Mix together. In another bowl lightly combine crabmeat, bread, green pepper and parsley. Pour liquid over crabmeat combination, toss lightly with your hands to blend, being careful not to break crabmeat lumps. Form into cakes and pan fry to crisp brown in Flavor Fry or butter. Can be used to stuff fish or shrimp or ramekins. Makes 15 large cakes.

THE LAMOTHE HOUSE
New Orleans, Louisiana

It is most unlikely that this creole jambalaya would be served at breakfast, the only meal served at this French Quarter inn. However, Mrs. Munson is happy to share her own family recipe for this great New Orleans delicacy.

CREOLE JAMBALAYA

2 tbs. shortening
1 large onion, minced
2 lbs. raw shrimp, peeled
  and rinsed
1/4 lb. ham, chopped
1 can (8 oz.) tomato paste
1/2 green pepper, chopped

1 bay leaf
1 sprig of thyme
1 tsp. salt
1/2 tsp. pepper
1 1/2 cups uncooked rice
2 cups water
2 tsp. parsley, finely chopped

Melt shortening in a heavy skillet and saute onions until light brown. Add shrimp and brown well; then add ham, green pepper, tomato paste and seasonings. Add rice and water and cover tightly. Cook over a low heat until rice is cooked and Jambalaya is dry. Stir with a fork once or twice to prevent burning. Just before serving, sprinkle with parsley. Serves 6.

AMERICAN HOTEL
Freehold, New Jersey

A most uncommon inn in a most uncommon setting. It has undoubtedly the finest collection of horse memorabilia anywhere. There are Currier & Ives and English horse prints and prized shoes, and tack from famous trotters and thoroughbreds of the last half century.

DEEP DISH CLAM PIE

3 cups diced clams	1½ qt. clam broth
2 cups diced carrots	2 tsp. salt
2 cups diced celery	1 tsp. white pepper
2 cups diced potatoes	2 tsp. accent
2 medium onions (chopped)	tarragon leaves—pinch
2 cups flour	Worcestershire sauce—to taste
½ lb. butter	

Melt butter in saucepan; add celery, onions, carrots, potatoes, seasonings. Cook until almost tender. Blend in white flour and continue to cook a few minutes. Add hot clam broth slowly until the mixture becomes thick. Finally add diced clams, stir gently until thoroughly mixed. Pour mixture into dough liner, (9 x 15 pan) cover top with dough strips; bake in 450 degree oven for 45 minutes.

The Algonquin has all of the country inn qualities for which we are searching in New York—and more. In a world of changes it has remained virtually unchanged. The Oak Room is the same as it was in the 20's and 30's when the famous Algonquin Roundtable was occupied by Dorothy Parker, Mark Connolly, Edna Ferber and Franklin P. Adams.

LOBSTER PROVENCALE au WILD RICE

2 lb. lobster, live
olive oil
1 tbs. sweet butter, melted
6 mushrooms, sliced
pinch garlic
1 onion, chopped

bayleaf
pinch rosemary
salt and pepper
2½ oz. sherry wine
4 fresh tomatoes, crushed

Steam or boil the lobster for 15 minutes. Remove the meat from the shell, cut in square pieces, and put in a sauce pan. Add a little olive oil, and next 7 ingredients. Cook the whole combination over medium heat, stirring occasionally, for about ten minutes. When the lobster is nice and brown, add the sherry and tomatoes. Let cook for another 20 minutes.

Serve on boiled wild rice, garnished with fresh chopped parsley. Serves 2.

1740 HOUSE
Lumberville, Pennsylvania

This inn on the banks of the Delaware River just above New Hope, Pennsylvania is continually being "discovered" by people from New York and Philadelphia. I like to spend part of my stay walking the tow path of the Delaware Canal.

FILLET OF FISH

4 fresh fish fillets
   (sole preferably)
1 cup bearnaise sauce
1 small onion, chopped

½ tsp. dill seed
thyme to taste
dash celery salt
2 tsp. parsley, chopped

Dry the fillets between paper towels and check for bones. Place in individual baking tins. Make a bearnaise sauce and add the remaining ingredients to it. Brush each fillet generously with the sauce and garnish with lemon slices and paprika. Bake in a 325 degree oven for 12 minutes.

ST. CLAIR INN
St. Clair, Michigan

The St. Clair looks like one of those tidy Tudor cottages that dot the English countryside...red brick and half-timbers. The dining room and terrace are just a few steps from the St. Clair River where the Great Lakes ships sail past day and night. It is an hour from Detroit on Interstate 94.

PAN FRIED PICKEREL

pickerel, (the size that filets out eight ounces per side)
salt

paprika flour (1 cup flour, 1 tbs. paprika mixed thoroughly)
vegetable shortening

Be sure all scales are removed. Wash thoroughly and make incision, with a sharp knife, on the skin side through the thickest part of the fish halfway to the tail end. Salt and dredge in paprika flour. Preheat vegetable shortening in frying pan and when hot place fish in skin side up. Brown on one side and turn. When both sides are brown (about 4 minutes per side) remove from pan and drain on paper towels. Serve with tartar sauce and lemon.

HARBORSIDE INN
Edgartown, Massachusetts

Pictorial Edgartown, on Martha's Vineyard Island, is famed for its houses of old whaling captains. The Harborside Inn occupies 6 of these serene, classic beauties. They form a sun-drenched courtyard which leads past the pool, down to the private docks. Embracing everything, the tang of the sea is mixed with the fragrance of those incredible flowers.

MARTHA'S VINEYARD SCALLOPED SCALLOPS

1 qt. Bay Scallops
6 medium potatoes sliced thinly
6 medium onions sliced thinly
salt and pepper

1 cup milk
¼ lb. butter
Small box of saltines crushed quite fine

Butter a pyrex or earthenware casserole.
Place in layers: Scallops (do not soak or wash—use fresh, if possible, right from the container), potatoes, onions, saltines, and a light dust of salt and pepper. Repeat layers until all ingredients are used. Pour milk evenly over all and dot with about six walnut-size pieces of butter. Place in pre-heated 325-350 degree oven uncovered for about an hour or until potatoes are cooked.

THE RED INN
Provincetown, Massachusetts

Although my Berkshire farmhouse does not overlook the waters of Provincetown Bay, I can recapture a few moments of some most enjoyable dinners there with this recipe for scalloped oysters.

SCALLOPED OYSTERS

1 pint Wellfleet oysters	½ tsp. pepper
1 cup cracker crumbs	¼ cup butter, melted
¼ tsp. salt	¼ to ½ cup light cream

To prepare oysters, empty them into a sieve, placed over a saucepan to catch the liquor. Lift them one by one and examine carefully for bits of shell. Mix salt, pepper and butter with the cracker crumbs. Spread a layer of the crumb mixture on the bottom of a shallow baking dish and cover with half the oysters. Spread another layer of crumb mixture and cover with the remaining oysters. Top with the remaining cracker crumbs. Add the oyster liquor and light cream until it can be seen in the crevices between the oysters. Bake in a 425 to 450 oven for 20 to 30 minutes.

COLD SPRING TAVERN
Santa Barbara, California

Here is a restaurant located at the bend of the road in the mountains north of Santa Barbara where one would fully expect to find banditos and renegades lurking behind every tree.

SALMA-CADO

3 ripe avocados
1/3 cup mayonnaise
½ cup sour cream
¼ tsp. seasonettes
sprinkling of celery salt
sprinkling of seasoned salt
1/3 cup hearts of celery,
    chopped fine
4½ oz. can tiny shrimp, rinsed
4¾ oz. can red salmon, drained

Cut the avocados in half lengthwise and remove the pit. Mix the remaining ingredients together and fill each avocado half with this mixture. Put a dab of sour cream on top and broil until bubbly. Serve on a plate right out of the shell. Serves 6.

Eggs & Cheese

BREAKFAST QUICHE
  Bradford Gardens Inn; Provincetown, Massachusetts
CHEESE FONDUE CLARKSON
  The Clarkson House; Lewiston, New York
CHEESE STRATA
  Hemlock Inn; Bryson City, North Carolina
GRITS AND CHEDDAR CHEESE
  Griswold Inn; Essex, Connecticut
EGGS DELMONICO
  The Carolina Inn; Chapel Hill, North Carolina
ENCANTADO ENCHILADAS
  Rancho Encantado; Santa Fe, New Mexico

BRADFORD GARDENS
Provincetown, Massachusetts

Breakfast is the only meal served by John Venner and Jim Logan at this tiny inn in Provincetown. John has at least 35 breakfast specialities.

BREAKFAST QUICHE

1 9'' pie crust, unbaked and
   in a deep pie plate
½ lb. bacon, coarsely chopped
½ cup scallions, tops and bottoms
1 cup fresh mushrooms, sliced

½ lb. Swiss cheese, sliced
½ pint heavy or medium cream
6 large eggs
sprinkling of salt, pepper
   and tarragon

Fry the bacon, scallions and mushrooms in a heavy skillet. Drain off all but 1 or 2 tablespoons of the liquid; spread the mixture over the pie crust. Cover evenly with sliced Swiss cheese. Blend the cream and eggs with a whisk and pour over the above. Sprinkle with the seasonings and bake in a 375 degree oven for 1 hour. Serve hot with toasted English muffins. Although the French do not serve quiche in the morning, it has become a favorite at Bradford Gardens' gourmet breakfasts.

CLARKSON HOUSE
Lewiston, New York

At the Clarkson House is a cannonball that was originally fired across the Niagara River at the Canadians during the War of 1812. Recently, one of their Canadian guests presented the cannonball to them saying they were returning it!

CHEESE FONDUE CLARKSON

2 cups Chablis wine
¼ cup cognac
1 tsp. salt
¼ tsp. nutmeg
¼ tsp. garlic powder

6 tbs. flour
10 oz. imported Swiss cheese,
   shredded
10 oz. gruyere cheese, shredded
French bread

Mix all of the ingredients together. Heat gently, stirring constantly, only until the cheese is melted and fondue slightly thick. Set aside until ready to serve. Then transfer the fondue to a fondue pot and set over a controlled flame. Cut French bread into bite size pieces and set aside to dunk into fondue.

It is very important that only these cheeses and only 10 ounces of each be used. Otherwise the fondue will be too stringy and not of the right consistency. This recipe can be easily multiplied or divided with unfailing success, depending upon the size party you are having. Served with a little wine and a large salad, this makes a delightful supper. Served alone, with cocktails, it's a fun hors d'oeuvre!

HEMLOCK INN
Bryson City, North Carolina

John and Ella Jo Shell's Hemlock Inn is high in the Great Smokies of western North Carolina. Guests in their dining room are seated around Lazy Susan tables and can gaze right into the gorgeous mountains.

CHEESE STRATA

bread	2 eggs
margarine	2½ cups milk
¾ lb. New York sharp cheese, grated	pinch of salt and pepper

After cutting away the crusts, line the bottom of a greased casserole with bread. Completely cover the layer of bread with cheese, then cover this with another layer of bread. Beat together eggs, milk and seasonings. Pour this mixture over the top of the bread and cheese layers, allowing it to soak through. Refrigerate overnight. Bake in a 325 degree oven for 45 minutes or until puffy.

THE GRISWOLD INN
Essex, Connecticut

Essex, Connecticut is famous for being the place where the first United States warship was built. It was attacked and burned during the War of 1812. It may seem unusual to be serving grits north of the Mason-Dixon Line, but this Griswold dish will taste good anywhere.

GRITS AND CHEDDAR CHEESE

1 lb. sharp cheddar cheese, grated
1 cup corngrits, cooked
½ cup margarine
3 tsp. salt
3 large eggs, beaten

Cook grits according to instructions on the package until smooth. Add the cheese and margarine and cool slightly. Add salt and carefully add the beaten eggs. Bake for one hour in a 275 to 300 degree oven.

47

THE CAROLINA INN
Chapel Hill, North Carolina

*At Chapel Hill in the late afternoon the lengthening shadows
create soft shapes and bring back distant memories.*

EGGS DELMONICO

1 cup margarine	½ cup sauterne
1 cup flour	6-7 hard cooked eggs, quartered
½ tsp. salt	4 oz. whole toasted almonds
½ tsp. Lawry's seasoned salt	½ cup pimentos, drained and cut
⅜ tsp. coarsely ground pepper	4 oz. cheddar cheese
¾ tsp. MSG	½-1 lb. whole frozen mushrooms
3½ cups whole milk	buttered bread crumbs

Make a roux of margarine and flour but do not brown. Add seasonings, sauterne and milk. Cook at low temperature while beating with a wire whip. Cook eggs at medium temperature; do not cook in a steamer. Place frozen mushrooms in a pan with margarine and cook over moderate heat for no more than 10 minutes. They should retain color and shape.

Combine cream sauce, eggs, mushrooms and the remaining ingredients lightly. Place in a casserole and top with buttered bread crumbs. Bake in a 300 degree oven until browned. Serves 6.

RANCHO ENCANTADO
Santa Fe, New Mexico

*I had this particular dish the morning I had breakfast at Rancho
Encantado. Although it does contain chilies, when prepared in
the right proportion, it is not uncomfortably over-seasoned. It
makes a perfect breakfast following an early morning desert
horseback ride at the Rancho.*

ENCANTADO ENCHILADAS

12 corn tortillas	1 cup diced onions
2 cups grated Longhorn cheese	

Put 2 tablespoons of cheese and 1 tablespoon of onion in middle of tortilla and roll it up.

Place enchiladas in baking pan and pour chili sauce over it. Sprinkle grated cheese on top. Place in oven and heat until sauce bubbles.

CHILI SAUCE

1 tbs. shortening	4 tbs. red chili powder (Chimayo Chili preferred)
2 tbs. flour	3 or 4 cups water

Melt shortening in pan, stir in flour and chili powder. Add water according to how thick you want your sauce. Bring to a boil and boil for 10 minutes. The longer you boil it—the hotter it gets.

Vegetables

BAKED BEANS
  Rabbit Hill Inn; Lower Waterford, Vermont
WESTERN STYLE CHILI BEANS
  Tanque Verde Ranch; Tucson, Arizona
CARROT CUSTARD
  Century Inn; Scenery Hill, Pennsylvania
WELSHFIELD GLAZED CARROTS
  Welshfield Inn; Burton, Ohio
SCALLOPED CABBAGE
  North Hero House; North Hero, Vermont
BAKED STUFFED CUCUMBERS
  Hound Ears Lodge; Blowing Rock, North Carolina

EGGPLANT SAUTE A LA REUBEN
  Ojai Valley Inn; Ojai, California
BAKED SUMMER SQUASH
  Lincklaen House; Cazenovia, New York
GREEN ONION PIE
  Park View Inn; Berkeley Springs, West Virginia
MUSHROOMS A LA SUTTER CREEK
  Sutter Creek Inn; Sutter Creek, California
CANDIED SWEET POTATOES WITH PEANUTS
  General Lewis Inn; Lewisburg, West Virginia

RABBIT HILL
Lower Waterford, Vermont

Lower Waterford, Vermont is known as "the White Village" and is said to be the most photographed village in New England. The view from the two balconies of the Rabbit Hill Inn includes the magnificent mountains of New Hampshire. It is just a few miles south of St. Johnsbury.

BAKED BEANS

1 qt. soldier beans
1 tsp. baking soda
1/3 cup molasses
2/3 cup Vermont maple syrup
1 cup sugar

1/8 tsp. ginger
1/8 tsp. pepper
1/3 lb. salt pork cut in ¾'' cubes
1/2 cup sugar
2 tsp. dry mustard

Soak beans overnight. Parboil for 10 minutes with 1 tsp. baking soda. Drain and rinse. Mix dry ingredients together. Place 1/3 of the dry ingredients and salt pork and beans in a crockery bean pot. Repeat this twice more, using all the beans, dry ingredients and salt pork. Pour molasses and maple syrup on top of the beans and cover with water. Cover, and place in a 350 degree oven for 2 hours, adding water after first hour. Reduce heat to 300 degrees, add ½ cup of sugar and continue baking until tender. Baking time can vary greatly depending on the beans, but do not overcook and allow to become mushy.

TANQUE VERDE RANCH
Tucson, Arizona

This is a southern Arizona guest ranch with an authentic history of pioneering, cattle rustling and Indian battles. When I prepare this recipe back home in New England, it brings back memories of real western cookouts, desert rides and the warm assurance of instant belonging, that were a part of my pleasant stay under the bright Arizona skies.

WESTERN STYLE CHILI BEANS

Two 1 lb. cans prepared baked beans (Western Style preferred)
½ pound crisp fried bacon, crumbled
8 drops Tabasco sauce
4 **tbs.** Worcestershire sauce
¼ **tbs.** chili powder
½ lb. grated cheddar cheese

Mix ingredients. Place in baking pan and sprinkle on top grated cheese. Bake in 350 degrees oven for about 30 min.—or until hot and cheese is melted.

CENTURY INN
Scenery Hill, Pennsylvania

The Century Inn was built previous to 1794 and is the oldest, continuously kept tavern on the National Pike most of which is known today as Route 40. It is filled with beautiful antiques and a fireplace that takes ten foot logs! Carrot Custard is just one of the wonderful country offerings.

CARROT CUSTARD

1 cup canned sliced carrots, coarsely chopped
1 cup bread crumbs
1 cup Cheddar cheese, grated
1 cup canned milk, diluted with ½ cup milk
6 tbs. butter, melted
2 eggs, beaten to hold their shape
1 tsp. salt

Mix ingredients together in mixer and pour into 7″ x 13″ x 2″ pan. Bake in 350 degree oven for 45 minutes to 1 hour.

WELSHFIELD INN
Burton, Ohio

At one time the Welshfield Inn was owned by the village post-master and was well known as a station for the underground rail-road. These country-style glazed carrots are one of the house specialties.

WELSHFIELD GLAZED CARROTS

1 medium can carrots, sliced or whole
1½ cups pineapple juice
2 tbs. orange concentrate
2 tbs. lemon juice
½ cup sugar

Drain the carrots and reserve the juice. Combine all of the ingredients in a saucepan and bring to a boil. Thicken with a mixture of 1 cup carrot juice and ¼ cup cornstarch. Add a little diced lemon and orange. Serve hot. Serves 6.

NORTH HERO HOUSE
North Hero, Vermont

North Hero and South Hero are two islands near Canada in the northern section of Lake Champlain. North Hero House, about forty-five minutes from Burlington, is right on the shores of the lake. The Scalloped Cabbage is one of the many recipes made from locally grown fresh vegetables each summer.

SCALLOPED CABBAGE

1 head cabbage, cut in 6-8 wedges
1 cup white sauce
½ cup sharp cheese, shredded
  corn flake crumbs
  salt, pepper

Cook cabbage in boiling salted water 10-12 minutes. Drain. Combine white sauce and shredded sharp cheese. Heat till cheese melts.
Place cabbage in baking pan. Pour sauce over cabbage, shake corn flake crumbs over entire pan. Salt and pepper to taste.
Bake in 350 degree oven for 30-35 minutes until hot and bubbly. Serves 4-6.

HOUND EARS LODGE
Blowing Rock, North Carolina

*Hound Ears is located in the southern highlands near the center
of a triangle formed by Blowing Rock, Boone and Linville.
During three seasons the golf is exceptional. In winter, bring
your skiis; the snow is beautiful.*

BAKED STUFFED CUCUMBERS

3 large oversize cucumbers	2 tsp. salt
1 medium onion, chopped	1 tsp. black pepper, freshly ground
¾ cup bread crumbs	bread crumbs
½ cup butter or margarine, melted	butter or margarine

Cut two of the large cucumbers in half crosswise, giving you four
"boats." Cut a slice lengthwise from the top of each boat. With a
melon ball cutter or teaspoon scoop out the pulp, being careful to
leave a wall about ¼ inch around all sides, including the cut end.
Peel the whole cucumber that is left, add to the pulp and chop all
medium fine. Add onion to the pulp and place all in a colander or
strainer to drain well. Add the bread crumbs, salt, pepper and butter or
margarine. Mix well, and stuff the cucumber boats with the mixture,
rounding the tops. Sprinkle more bread crumbs over each top, spoon
some of the extra melted butter or margarine over the crumbs and dust
each with paprika.
Place the boats in a shallow baking pan, add enough water to cover the
bottom of the pan and bake for 1 hour at oven temperature of 300
degrees. Serves four.

OJAI VALLEY INN
Ojai, California

Golf is the name of the game at the Ojai Valley Inn—with tennis and riding as extracurricular fun. It's just far enough away from Los Angeles to be out of the crowd and smog. The menu is quite sophisticated including this unusual treatment of eggplant which grows profusely in this part of Southern California.

EGGPLANT SAUTE A LA REUBEN

1 medium eggplant
2 dozen mushroom caps (medium size)
  butter
  flour
1½ cups hollandaise sauce

Saute the mushroom caps in butter and set aside. Peel the eggplant and slice lengthwise; dredge in flour and saute in butter until golden brown and tender. Place the mushroom caps on the eggplant and cover with hollandaise sauce. Set in a salamander to glaze.

LINCKLAEN HOUSE
Cazenovia, New York

The graceful yellow Lincklaen House, with its impressive balustrade, was built by the founder of Cazenovia in 1835, and the passing years have enhanced its beauty. We enjoy the snowy white linens, shining silver, Williamsburg chandeliers, crackling fireplaces, painted wood panels and heaps of family style cooking, including pork roast, applesauce and popovers.

BAKED SUMMER SQUASH

3 lbs. small yellow squash (6 cups)
¼ cup butter
  salt and pepper to taste
1½ cups onion, chopped

½ cup milk
2 large eggs
½ cup cracker crumbs
  melted butter

Wash, don't peel squash. Cut into small pieces and cook in salted water until tender. Don't overcook. Drain and pour squash into baking dish immediately. Add butter, then mix salt, pepper and onions. Combine milk and eggs and mix well with squash. Top with a little melted butter and cracker crumbs. Bake for 20 minutes or until brown in a 450 degree oven. Personally, I could make a meal of this along with a green salad. It's great for a night when the entree is on the light side.

THE COUNTRY INN
Berkeley Springs, West Virginia

Here's an inn that stands firmly astride north and south ... a sort of Mason-Dixon Line of its very own. The menu reflects different preferences in food as well but this Green Onion pie would be at home in New England and in New Orleans. Try it on some of your best friends some night.

GREEN ONION PIE

1 unbaked pie shell
3 cups green onions, tops and
    bottoms
3 tbs. butter
2 eggs

½ cup sharp cheese, grated or
    ½ cup crumbled bacon
½ cup cream
½ tsp. salt
    dash of pepper

Slice the green onions and saute until tender. Arrange them in an unbaked pie shell. Beat eggs slightly; stir in remaining ingredients. Pour over the onions and bake in a 425 degree oven for 18 to 20 minutes. It is done when well browned and when a metal knife inserted halfway between center and edge comes out clean. Serves 4 to 6.

The house belongs in New England yet we were in the California gold rush country. Honeysuckle, rose, chintz spreads, velvet chairs, a kitchen with a huge New Hampshire fireplace and the purtiest innkeeper in five counties.

MUSHROOMS A LA SUTTER CREEK

8 very large mushrooms	1½ tbs. steak sauce
1 cup ground flank steak	1 tsp. salt
¼ cup chopped onions	freshly ground pepper
¼ cup chopped celery (or water	chives
chestnuts)	scrambled eggs

Wash and remove stems from mushrooms. Set aside. Combine ground flank steak, very finely chopped onions and celery (or water chestnuts), steak sauce, salt, and freshly ground pepper.
Divide meat mixture into 8 equal portions and pack into mushrooms. Place mushrooms meat side down in baking dish or pan. Sprinkle mushrooms with salt. Bake at 375 degrees for 15 to 20 minutes and serve with scrambled eggs sprinkled with fresh chives for a different breakfast.

I love candied sweet potatoes and I particularly love the way they are served at the General Lewis, which is in one of the historical towns in Southeast West Virginia.

CANDIED SWEET POTATOES WITH PEANUTS

6 medium sweet potatoes	4 tbs. butter
½ cup brown sugar	½ tsp. salt
1 cup boiling water	2 tsp. chopped peanuts

Pare and slice the potatoes. Make a syrup of sugar, water, butter and salt. Put potatoes in a shallow baking dish and pour syrup over them. Bake in a slow oven for 1 hour or until candied. Before taking them from the oven, sprinkle with chopped peanuts and brown lightly.

Salads

JOHN HANCOCK INN SALAD DRESSING
   The John Hancock Inn; Hancock, New Hampshire
EMERALD SALAD
   Snowbird Mountain Lodge; Robbinsville, North Carolina
TEA GARDEN SALAD
   Boone Tavern Hotel; Berea, Kentucky
SPINACH SALAD
   The Tavern; New Wilmington, Pennsylvania
DANISH COLD POTATO SALAD
   Kilravock Inn; Litchfield, Connecticut

JOHN HANCOCK INN
Hancock, New Hampshire

The John Hancock is the oldest inn in New Hampshire and is located in the beautiful Mt. Monadnock region, near the state's southern border. Hancock is a very sequestered village with many New England houses set among the trees. The inn is the center of community activity.

JOHN HANCOCK INN SALAD DRESSING

4 eggs
3 cups salad oil
½ tsp. oregano
1 tsp. salt
1 tsp. white pepper

½ tsp. garlic powder
juice of one lemon
2 oz. can anchovies, chopped fine
½ cup cider vinegar
½ cup Parmesan cheese

Using mixer or hand beater, whip eggs, gradually adding oil. Then add seasonings. Yields one quart.

SNOWBIRD MOUNTAIN LODGE
Robbinsville, North Carolina

Snowbird Mountain Lodge sits atop its own mountain in the Great Smokies, and good walking and hiking trails lead from the lodge in almost every direction. This emerald salad reminds me of the fresh vibrant colors of a North Carolina springtime.

EMERALD SALAD

2 tbs. gelatin	dash of onion juice (optional)
1 cup cold wtter	1 can (medium size) pineapple,
1 cup sugar	crushed with juice
½ cup water	1 cup nuts, finely chopped
1/3 cup vinegar	1 cup sweet pickles, sliced thin
	½ cup celery, chopped

Dissolve the gelatin in cold water and soak for 5 minutes. Cook sugar, water and vinegar to a thin syrup. Add the gelatin mixture to the hot, but not boiling, syrup and stir until dissolved. Pour into a serving dish or a mold and allow to cool. When it begins to set add the remaining ingredients. Let this set for two hours or until firm. Serve on lettuce with mayonnaise.

BOONE TAVERN HOTEL
Berea, Kentucky

This is a "neat as a pin" Kentucky country inn staffed for the most part by cheerful, well-trained, eager and alert students of Berea College, many of whom are hotel management majors. They alone are worth the visit. The inn has the charm of an earlier era, but is completely modern in its facilities and service.

TEA GARDEN SALAD

1 pkg. orange gelatin	1 11 oz. can mandarin orange
1 cup hot freshly made black tea	sections
1 cup juice drained from oranges	1 8 oz. can crushed pineapple
and pineapple	1 8 oz. can water chestnuts

DRESSING:
1 cup whipped cream dressing (Fold ½ cup mayonnaise into 1 cup stiffly whipped cream.)
Grated rind of 1 orange
Pinch of mace

Dissolve gelatin in hot tea. Add cup of juice from Mandarin oranges and pineapple. (Add regular orange juice to fill cup if needed.) Stir. Place gelatin in refrigerator until it has thickened considerably. Drain and cut water chestnuts into small slices. Add chestnuts, pineapple, and orange sections to gelatin.
Spoon mixture into well-oiled molds. Refrigerate until set. Mix whipped cream dressing with orange rind and mace. Serve on top of salad. This recipe is from one of three of manager Dick Hougen's excellent cookbooks, ''Cooking with Hougen,'' with recipes from the Boone Tavern Hotel.

THE TAVERN
New Wilmington, Pennsylvania

Located in the Amish country of western Pennsylvania, the Tavern at New Wilmington still preserves the country traditions of really huge portions at each meal. This spinach tastes best if you get it from your own garden.

SPINACH SALAD

4 cups fresh spinach	½ to 1 cup mayonnaise
½ cup celery, diced	1 tsp. vinegar
½ cup onion, grated	½ tsp. salt
3 hard-boiled eggs, chopped	dash of Tabasco sauce
¾ cup Old English sharp cheese	

Remove the stems from the spinach. Mix mayonnaise, vinegar, salt and Tabasco and add to the celery, onion, eggs and cheese. Lastly, add the spinach to the above mixture carefully to avoid bruising the leaves. For best results mix all but eggs and spinach and refrigerate overnight.

KILRAVOCK INN
Litchfield, Connecticut

The Kilravock is an elegant country inn that is like an English or Scottish manor house. It's a short drive from New York. I've served Lis Hoyt's Danish Cold Potato Salad many times with great success.

DANISH COLD POTATO SALAD

2 lbs. firm, boiled potatoes, sliced ¼ inch thick	½ tsp. white pepper
	1 small onion, grated
7 oz. mayonnaise	3 oz. whipping cream
1 tsp. dry mustard	chopped chives, sliced radishes
juice of ½ lemon	and watercress

Season the mayonnaise with mustard, lemon juice, pepper and onion. Whip the cream until stiff and mix into the seasoned mayonnaise. Blend the dressing with the sliced potatoes and chill. Serve garnished with chives, radishes and watercress. Serves 6.

Breads

APPLE-WHEAT BREAD
  Bird and Bottle Inn; Garrison, New York
ALL NATURAL BANANA NUT BREAD
  The Wells Wood; Plainfield, New Hampshire
STEAMED BOSTON BROWN BREAD
  Longfellow's Wayside Inn; South Sudbury, Massachusetts
PUMPKIN BREAD
  Mountain View Inn; Norfolk, Connecticut
SPICE BREAD
  Larchwood Inn; Wakefield, Rhode Island
IRENE'S WHITE BREAD
  Wayside Inn; Middletown, Virginia
APPLE MUFFINS
  Graves Mountain Lodge; Syria, Virginia
JOHNNY CAKE
  Milford House, South Milford, Nova Scotia
TEA BISCUITS
  The Gate House; Niagara-on-the-Lake, Ontario
SOUR CREAM COFFEE CAKE
  Sterling Inn; South Sterling, Pennsylvania
SILVER DOLLAR PANCAKES
  Heritage House; Little River, California

THE BIRD AND BOTTLE
Garrison, New York

Shades of Benedict Arnold, George Washington, Major Andre and Israel Putnam! The chances are that the woods and streams around this ancient hostelry have seen all of these famous colonial figures and many more. It has a delightful conspiratorial air about it with low ceilings, flickering candles and most elegant table settings.

APPLE-WHEAT BREAD

½ cup butter or margarine, melted
1½ cups brown sugar, firmly packed
2 eggs

2 cups unbleached,
    all-purpose flour
2 tbs. baking powder
1 tsp. salt
1½ cups whole wheat flour
½ cup nonfat dry milk
½ cup rolled oats
½ cup wheat germ
1 cup chopped nuts
1 cup chopped dates or raisins
1½ cups apple, unpeeled,
    cored and chopped
1¾ cups milk

Preheat oven to 350 degrees. Grease one large or two small loaf pans. Mix melted butter and brown sugar together and beat in eggs. Sift all-purpose flour, baking powder and salt into another bowl; stir in whole wheat flour, dry milk, oats and wheat germ. Then add nuts, dates and apple. Add flour mixture to egg mixture about a third at a time, alternating with the milk. Stir thoroughly after each addition. Batter will be stiff and difficult to stir. Fill a loaf pan ¾ full with the dough and bake for 1 hour and 10 minutes. If using muffin tins, bake for 45 minutes. When done, remove from oven and place on wire rack to cool for 10 minutes. Remove loaf from pan and place on rack to cool.

WELLS WOOD
Plainfield, New Hampshire

At Wells Wood I expect the unexpected. For one thing, Rosalind Wells might well be singing "The Bell Song" from Lakme while preparing this unusual banana bread. At the same time guests in the garden or dining room would be enjoying the same view of Mt. Ascutney which inspired Maxfield Parrish.

WELLS WOOD ALL NATURAL BANANA NUT BREAD

3/4 cup oil
 1 cup brown sugar
 2 tbs. honey
2/3 cup milk
 4 very ripe bananas
 3 large eggs
 2 cups whole wheat flour
 1 tsp. baking soda
 1 tsp. vanilla
3/4 cup walnuts, coarsely chopped
1/4 cup mixed nuts, chopped

Cream sugar, oil and honey; add milk, bananas and eggs. In a separate bowl, combine the dry ingredients, then slowly add them to the banana mixture. Add more milk if the mixture seems too thick. Fold in nuts and the vanilla. Bake in a greased bundt pan in a 350 degree oven for one hour.

LONGFELLOW'S WAYSIDE INN
South Sudbury, Massachusetts

"As ancient is this hostelry as any in the land may be." So wrote Longfellow of the Wayside Inn in 1863 . Today this old inn, as the result of continual restoration and preservation, is one of the most beloved in the world. Its antiques are price- less pieces, much admired by collectors everywhere. Further- more, I find it highly convenient to stay there when visiting Boston.

PUMPKIN MUFFINS

1 cup raisins ⎰ soak together while measuring
½ cup water ⎱ other ingredients

1 cup canned pumpkin	¾ tsp. cloves
1 cup plus 4 tbs. sugar	¾ tsp. cinnamon
2 eggs	½ cup plus 2 tbs. cooking oil
1 tsp. salt	1¾ cups flour
½ tsp. soda	1½ tsp. baking powder

Mix above ingredients together and add half of water-raisin mixture. Mix well and add remaining water-raisin mixture. Mix until smooth and drop into well-greased muffin or cup cake pans. Bake at 400-425 degrees for about 15 minutes, until top springs back when pressed with fingers. Makes about a dozen large muffins or one large loaf.

MOUNTAIN VIEW INN
Norfolk, Connecticut

Among my lasting impressions of the Mountain View is the tantilizing aroma of the Sweet Breads Viennoise, Roast Beef, Sauerbraten, and the quite different pumpkin bread which is included below. It has home-size bedrooms and many fireplaces. Also an unusual collection of clocks.

PUMPKIN BREAD

4½ ozs. shortening
1¼ lb. sugar
1½ lb. flour
¾ lb. nuts (optional)
6 eggs

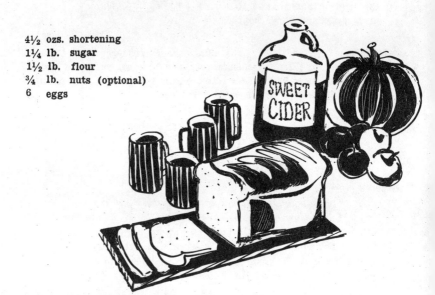

1 lb. 4 oz. pumpkin
½ pint water
  (more if batter is too thick)
¾ tsp. baking powder
2¼ tsp. salt

2½ tsp. baking soda
¾ tsp. ground cloves
1 1/3 tsp. ginger

Cream shortening and add sugar until ball is formed. Add eggs and pumpkin and mix well. Add half the flour and mix well. Then add spices, baking soda and powder to remainder and mix to batter with water. Add nuts if desired. Bake in 425 degree oven until bread has crowned nicely. Reduce oven to 325 degrees and bake another 40 minutes. Test frequently with toothpick or cake tester. Remove from oven and let set 5 minutes. Turn out on rack or waxed paper. Bread will be moist. Makes 4 loaves which may be frozen.

LARCHWOOD INN
Wakefield, Rhode Island

The balustrade-topped Larchwood suns itself sedately on the broad green lawns, musing, no doubt, about the passage of time and events in historic southern Rhode Island. Inside, however, it's all hustle and bustle as this Scots-inspired inn prepares to satisfy many hungry lads and lassies.

SPICE BREAD

2¼ cups boiling water
1 cup mincemeat
4 cups sifted flour
4 tsp. baking soda
1 tsp. cinnamon
2 cups sugar

¼ cup melted shortening
2 eggs
1 cup broken nut meats
2 cups bran flakes
1 cup corn flakes
2 tsp. salt

Pour boiling water over mincemeat. Cool this mixture and add flour, soda, cinnamon, salt and sugar. Stir well. Then add shortening, eggs and mix well. Fold nut meats, cornflakes and bran flakes into mixture and bake in greased loaf pan for an hour at 350 degrees. Makes 2 loaves. This will make a great holiday snack and it's very good when served with hot chocolate on brisk evenings too. As a change of pace I have eaten a slice of this with a dollop of ice cream.

WAYSIDE INN
Middletown, Virginia

The history of the Wayside extends into three centuries and is located at the northern end of the wonderous Shenandoah Valley. It is just about an hour west of Washington and in the summertime the combination of dinner and drama at the Wayside Theatre finds favor with many D.C. escapees.

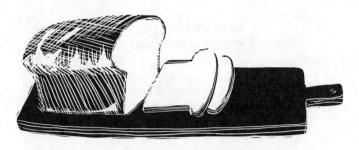

IRENE'S WHITE BREAD

2 cups milk, scalded
2 eggs, lightly beaten
½ tsp. salt
3 tbs. sugar

2 yeast cakes
3 cups flour
2 tbsp. shortening, melted
melted shortening

Heat milk, salt and sugar. Cool to lukewarm. Dissolve yeast in milk mixture. Add eggs. Beat thoroughly. Gradually stir in flour to make dough that handles easily. Turn onto floured board and knead until smooth, adding more flour if needed. Place dough in greased bowl and brush with two tablespoons of melted shortening, cover and let rise 2-3 hours until doubled in bulk. Then punch down, knead and shape into loaves. Place loaves in well-greased pans, brush with melted shortening cover and allow to rise until double in bulk. Bake in hot oven, 375 degrees, about 20 minutes, reduce heat to 350 degrees and bake about 45 minutes longer. Makes approximately 2 loaves.

GRAVES MOUNTAIN LODGE
Syria, Virginia

Syria, Virginia is located up against the eastern slopes of the Blue Ridge Mountains. The Graves Family has been "keeping" travelers there since before the War Between The States, and today its family-style food brings many people up this little country road between the farm fields. These Baked Apples are typical of the farm fare which is served there everyday.

APPLE MUFFINS

1 egg
1 cup milk
¼ cup butter
1 cup apples, grated

¼ cup sugar
2 cups flour
3 tsp. baking powder
1 tsp. salt
½ tsp. cinnamon

Mix together the first four ingredients. Add the remaining ingredients. Pour the batter into greased muffin tins and bake in a 400 degree oven for 20 to 25 minutes.

MILFORD HOUSE
South Milford, Nova Scotia

When guests leave this hideaway inn tucked away in the forests of southern Nova Scotia, everyone remaining stands on the front porch and waves them goodby. This Johnny Cake brings back many fond memories for me.

JOHNNY CAKE

½ cup sugar
3 tbs. butter, melted
1 egg
1 cup milk
1 cup yellow cornmeal

1 cup flour
1 tsp. cream of tartar
½ tsp. soda
1 tsp. salt

Lightly mix together all of the ingredients. Bake in a square baking pan in a 350 degree oven. Cut into squares and serve hot.

THE GATE HOUSE
Niagara-on-the-Lake, Ontario

The Gate House is a "neat-as-a-pin" Canadian inn in a truly fetching town near Niagara Falls, New York, USA. These tea biscuits are typical of their Canadian menu.

TEA BISCUITS

2 cups all-purpose flour
2 tbs. sugar
½ tsp. salt
3 tsp. baking powder

3 tbs. butter
1 egg
½ cup milk

Sift dry ingredients and add butter. Beat the egg and milk together and add to dry ingredients. These can be baked in muffin tins or rolled to a ¾ to 1 inch thickness and cut with a cookie cutter, then placed on a cookie sheet to bake. If you wish to use these biscuits as shortcakes, reheat them before serving. Cut them in half and cover one half with a layer of fresh fruit, then the second half of the biscuit and another layer of fruit. Top with whipped cream or serve with table cream. They are delicious with stewed rhubarb as well as fresh strawberries, peaches or raspberries. I've also tried adding floured raisins to the recipe and serving them hot with homemade jams.

I had to get lost before I could find this remarkably hospitable inn in the Pennsylvania Pocono mountains. This Sour Cream Coffee Cake is served there almost every morning. Mine turned out very well.

SOUR CREAM COFFEE CAKE

2 cups sour cream	2 tsp. baking powder
6 eggs	½ tsp. baking soda
2 cups flour	¼ tsp. salt
2 cups sugar	cinnamon

Beat eggs and sour cream well. Sift the flour before measuring, then resift with sugar, baking powder, soda and salt. Add the dry ingredients to egg mixture and beat until smooth. Spread the dough in a greased 8x10 inch pan. Bake at 350 degrees for 25 minutes. While hot, sprinkle with cinnamon. Serve warm.

HERITAGE HOUSE
Little River, California

This inn is just made for those who like a generous dollop of New England to temper the wild northern California coast! The guest cottages, all artfully placed with a sea view, were inspired by early area buildings. It's a short drive to the great Redwood Forests.

SILVER DOLLAR PANCAKES

1 cup flour	1 egg
1 tsp. sugar	¾ cup canned milk
1 tsp. baking powder	½ cup water
½ tsp. salt	2 tbs. melted butter

Mix dry ingredients, beat egg, milk and water. Add to dry ingredients. Whip well, adding melted butter. Pour enough batter on the griddle to cover a silver dollar. Make as many as possible at one time. Serve by the plateful.

At first I thought this recipe was just like every other pancake formula. Then I noticed that canned milk is specified. I tested it for myself and discovered a significant difference in lightness.

Desserts

AUNT MARY'S INDIAN MEAL PUDDING
The Melrose Inn; Harwichport, Massachusetts
BAKED INDIAN PUDDING
Lord Jeffrey Inn; Amherst, Massachusetts
HARVEST PUDDING
Whitehall Inn; Camden, Maine
NANTUCKET CHRISTMAS PUDDING
Jared Coffin House; Nantucket; Island, Massachusetts
MOCHA MOUSSE
Candlewyck Inn; Green Lane, Pennsylvaina
FUDGE CAKE
The Whistling Oyster; Ogunquit, Maine
ROSS' CHOCOLATE CAKE
Kilmuir Place; Northeast Margaree, Nova Scotia
BOULDERS MINCEMEAT BARS
The Boulders Inn; New Preston, Connecticut
OAT CAKES
Inverary Inn; Baddeck, Nova Scotia
RUM SQUARES
Woodbound Inn; Jaffrey, New Hampshire
RAISIN AND NUT BARS
Drovers Inn; Wellsburg, West Virginia
SPICE SQUARES WITH LEMON SAUCE
Kedron Valley Inn; South Woodstock, Vermont
FROZEN LEMON PIE
New England Inn; Intervale, New Hampshire
BUTTERMILK PIE
Lakeview Lodge; Roanoke, Virginia
HEAVENLY PIE
Stafford's-in-the-Field, Chocorua, New Hampshire
MAPLE CHIFFON PIE
Green Mountain Inn; Stowe, Vermont
MOLASSES COCONUT PIE
Moselem Springs Inn; Moselem Springs, Pennsylvania
PECAN PIE
Kimberton Country House; Kimberton, Pennsylvania
SHAKER SUGAR PIE
The Golden Lamb; Lebanon, Ohio
BLUEBERRY FRITTERS
Bethel Inn; Bethel, Maine
FRESH PEACH ICE CREAM
Jordan Pond House; Seal Harbor, Maine
MELON IN RUM-LIME SAUCE
Three Village Inn; Stony Brook, New York

THE MELROSE INN
Harwichport, Massachusetts

The Harwiches are real picture-book Cape Cod. The Melrose Inn faces a tree-shaded street, but it's just a step or two down to the Inn's private beach on Nantucket Sound where, in addition to jogging and suntanning, there's swimming in those warm southern waters.

AUNT MARY'S INDIAN MEAL PUDDING

1 qt. milk	3 tbs. corn meal
1 cup molasses, scant (light)	1 tsp. ginger
½ cup cold water	1 egg, beaten
½ cup seedless raisins	

Scald 3 cups of the milk in double boiler. Add corn meal after wetting it with a little water. Then add molasses, ginger, rest of milk and water, beaten egg and raisins. Boil until separated, curdled or wheyed. Bake in a well buttered pudding dish for 2½ hours in a 350 degree oven. Serve hot with cream or ice cream.

Here is a Colonial recipe if I ever saw one. It utilizes ingredients that were brought in to Cape Cod or grown there during the 18th Century. Although it is called Indian Pudding, I'm rather certain that all the Indians did with this concoction was to eat it. It definitely has the touch of a resourceful Cape Cod housewife.

THE LORD JEFFERY INN

"The Lord Jeff" as it is called by all of the town and gown types in Amherst is a sizeable, busy, bustling college town inn. The menu contains many New England specialties and nothing could be more New England than Baked Indian Pudding. I found that this is particularly appropriate on Saturday nights when I can't get to the Lord Jeff myself.

BAKED INDIAN PUDDING

1 cup yellow granulated corn meal
½ cup black molasses
¼ cup granulated sugar
¼ cup lard or butter

¼ tsp. salt
¼ tsp. baking soda
2 eggs
1½ qts. hot milk

Mix the first seven ingredients thoroughly with one half of the above hot milk (¾ quart) and bake in a very hot oven until the mixture boils. Then stir in the remaining hot milk and bake in a well-greased stone crock at a low oven temperature for five to seven hours. Makes a half gallon.

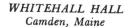

WHITEHALL HALL
Camden, Maine

Camden is one of the prettiest towns on the Maine coast. It is perhaps best known for being the home of Edna St. Vincent Millay and the site of the Whitehall Inn. If you are feeling "New Englandy" try this.

HARVEST PUDDING

3½ cups tart apples, sliced
½ cup raisins
¾ cup sugar
½ tsp. cinnamon
¼ tsp. nutmeg
½ cup walnuts
¼ tsp. salt
1 tsp. butter
1 tsp. lemon juice

BATTER TOPPING:
½ cup sugar
1¼ cups flour
1 tsp. baking powder
¼ tsp. salt
½ cup milk
1 egg
3 tbs. butter or margarine, melted
¼ cup walnuts

Place apples and raisins in a well-greased 8x13 baking pan. Combine next five ingredients and sprinkle over the fruit. Dot with butter and lemon juice. For batter topping, sift dry ingredients together. Combine milk, eggs and butter and add dry ingredients to this mixture. Mix until smooth. Pour over the apples and raisins, then sprinkle with more walnuts. Bake in a 375 degree oven for 30 minutes. Serve with ice cream or whipped cream topped with cinnamon. Serves 8.

JARED COFFIN HOUSE
Nantucket Island, Massachusetts

Nantucket, 30 miles off Cape Cod, is an island frozen in time. It's been spared the excesses of the Victorian age and the modern developer. The 3-story, red brick Jared Coffin House is a meticulous example of the early 19th Century Greek revival. The interior abounds with Chippendale, Sheraton and Federal. It's open year-round and Christmas is a joyous season.

NANTUCKET CHRISTMAS PUDDING

¼ cup all purpose flour
1½ tsp. all spice
¾ tsp. each nutmeg and cinnamon
½ tsp. each ginger and salt
2 cups raisins
1½ cups currants
¼ cup prunes, chopped
1 cup candied orange peel, chopped

1 cup candied lemon peel, chopped
2 tsp. lemon rind, grated
1¾ cup brown sugar
3 cups dry bread crumbs
6 oz. suet, finely ground
4 eggs, beaten
¼ cup cider

Sift together the flour and spices. Stir in fruits, sugar, bread crumbs and suet. Add the eggs and cider. Stir well.

Turn into greased 1½ quart mold. Cover with greased foil: Tie. Steam 5 hours. Cool. Unmold. Saturate with brandy or substitute. Store sealed—age 1 to 12 months.
To serve — Steam 1 hour, top with cranberry honey or warm lemon sauce. Serves 12.

CANDLEWYCK INN
Green Lane, Pennsylvania

Dating back to 1744, Candlewyck, the inn of the many glowing candles, nestles among the rolling hills of the Perkiomen Valley about an hour north of Philadelphia. It is an exemplary blend of food and atmosphere. The dessert below is one of my preferences.

MOCHA MOUSSE

8 oz. cream cheese
3 eggs
6 oz. sweet chocolate
1 envelope or 1 tbs. gelatin
2 tbs. cold water

1 pkg. lady fingers
1 cup brown sugar
1 tsp. vanilla
1½ cups heavy cream
1 tsp. instant coffee

Let cream cheese soften at room temperature. Separate 3 eggs; let stand half hour at room temperature. Melt chocolate. Soften gelatin in cup with cold water. Place cup in skillet of simmering water until gelatin dissolves. Line bottom and sides of 9'' spring form pan with split lady fingers. Beat egg whites until stiff. Blend in ½ cup brown sugar a little at a time. Add vanilla and continue beating until glossy; set aside.

Whip cream and set aside. Beat cream cheese until fluffy; stir in remaining sugar a little at a time. Flavor with instant coffee. Add egg yolks one at a time, beating after each addition. Stir in chocolate and gelatin. Fold in egg whites and cream. Pour into pan. Chill in refrigerator 2 hours or overnight. Garnish with rosettes of whipped cream. Serves 12.

WHISTLING OYSTER
Ogunquit, Maine

I would seek out the Whistling Oyster even if it were'nt perched on the edge of Perkins Cove in Ogunquit, with a perfect view of the drawbridge, and within speaking distance of the myriad of boats in the snug harbor. Even if it didn't have an exceptional gift shop, it would have to be the Lobster Provencale and this Fudge Cake.

FUDGE CAKE

2 cups cake flour
1 tsp. baking soda (sifted in
    with flour
½ cup butter
1 teaspoon vanilla

2 cups sifted brown sugar
2 eggs
4 squares of melted chocolate
1 cup soured milk

Cream shortening. Add sifted sugar, then add eggs mixing thoroughly after each addition. Next add melted chocolate. Add flour and baking soda mixture alternately with milk. Bake in layer cake pans in a 350 degree oven for 25 minutes.

CHOCOLATE FILLING

2 squares chocolate
1 cup milk
2 tbsp. flour
⅜ cup sugar

1 tbsp. cornstarch
¼ tbsp. salt
1 tbsp. butter
1 tbsp. vanilla

Melt chocolate in top part of double boiler. Add milk gradually and continue beating. Mix sugar, flour, cornstarch and salt. Then pour on a portion of the hot milk and chocolate. Add butter and vanilla. Return all to double boiler. Stir and cook until thickened.

CHOCOLATE FUDGE FROSTING

5 squares melted chocolate
1½ cups confectioner's sugar
½ cup butter

Cream butter, add sugar gradually.
Then add chocolate after cooled.
Frosting can be brought to any desired consistency by adding milk
and ½ teaspoon of vanilla.
When layer cakes have cooled, fill
with chocolate filling and frost.

I first saw this chocolate cake in the wonderously warm and inviting kitchen of the Kilmuir Place in Margaree, Cape Breton, Nova Scotia. Mrs. Ross Taylor had just finished the icing and it was a sight to behold. With the first bite I could only wish that Cape Breton were five hundred miles closer to the Berkshires.

ROSS' CHOCOLATE CAKE

1 cup shortening	5 eggs
2 cups sugar	2¼ cups cake flour, sifted
2 tsp. vanilla	1 tsp. soda
4 1 oz. squares chocolate,	1 tsp. salt
unsweetened, melted	1 cup sour milk or buttermilk

Cream well the shortening and sugar, add vanilla, melted chocolate and eggs. Mix well. Sift together dry ingredients, add to the first mixture alternately with the sour milk and stir until smooth. Pour into 2 round 9" cake tins. Bake in a 350 degree oven for 30-35 minutes, or until done.

FROSTING

2 cups sugar	½ cup margarine
⅓ cup cocoa	¼ tsp. salt
½ cup milk	1 tsp. vanilla

Bring first 5 ingredients to a rolling boil, and boil 2 minutes. Remove from stove. When cool, add vanilla and beat.

THE BOULDERS
New Preston, Connecticut

Fresh air, green mountains and a wind swept lake. Seventy-five years ago a spacious home on 250 acres; today the third generation extends a welcome for a country holiday. Swimming, boating, hiking, resting, skiing and eating.

BOULDERS MINCEMEAT BARS

¼ cup shortening	¾ cup mincemeat
¾ cup sugar	½ tsp. cinnamon
1½ cup sifted flour	¼ tsp. soda
½ tsp. salt	½ cup crushed pineapple, undrained
2 eggs well beaten	½ cup chopped walnuts

Cream shortening, gradually add sugar. Sift together dry ingredients. Beat eggs, add mincemeat, crushed pineapple and walnuts, mix well. Blend in dry ingredients gradually, mix thoroughly. Turn into greased 15 x 10 shallow pan. Bake at 350 degrees for 20-25 minutes. Cool slightly. Ice.

ICING

2 cups sifted confectioners sugar
2 tbls. hot pineapple juice

Combine over hot water and mix well. Add more sugar if necessary. Spread while hot. When set, cut in squares.

INVERARY INN
Baddeck, Nova Scotia

Overlooking Bras D'or in Baddeck, Nova Scotia, the Inverary is as enticing a bit of Scotland as could be found east of Edinburgh. These oat cakes take me back to a beautiful summer morning with both the water and sky a vivid Cape Breton blue.

OAT CAKES

6 cups rolled oats
3 cups flour, white
1 cup sugar, white
½ tsp. soda
1 tsp. salt
1 lb. shortening, or lard
water to mix

Mix dry ingredients. Cut in shortening and add water. Roll out to ¼ inch thick in graham flour and cut in 3x3 squares. Bake in 375 degree oven for 30 minutes.

WOODBOUND INN
Jaffrey, New Hampshire

I traveled deep into the woods to find this family resort-inn tucked away in the New Hampshire forest. There is indoor and outdoor activity for almost every month of the year, including cross-country skiing. That's when these rum squares taste so good.

RUM SQUARES

DOUGH:

1 cup flour
¼ cup sugar

4 tbs. margarine
1 egg

FROSTING:

3 cups confectioners' sugar

¼ cup melted butter
Rum or milk

FILLING:

3 eggs
1¾ cups brown sugar
1½ cups coconut
1 cup pecans or walnuts, chopped

3 tbs. flour
¾ tsp. baking powder
1 tsp. vanilla
½ tsp. salt

Mix the ingredients for dough together and spread in a jelly roll pan. Bake in a moderate oven long enough to form a slight crust, about 8 minutes. Remove from the oven and cool. Mix together the ingredients for the filling and pour over the dough. Finish baking until firm in the center. Mix together the ingredients for the frosting, adding enough rum to make the frosting spreadable. Substitute milk if you do not wish a rum flavor. Frost and cut into squares.

DROVERS INN
Wellsburg, West Virginia

Over a century ago the road in front of the Drovers Inn was a principal route for drovers moving their stock across the toll pike from Pennsylvania to Ohio. At the Drovers Inn they could obtain not only lodging and food for themselves but fodder for their livestock. Wellsburg, West Virginia is located in a funny little part of the mountaineer state that sticks up between Ohio and Pennsylvania. It's a few miles north of Wheeling.

RAISIN AND NUT BARS

½ lb. raisins
1 cup water
½ cup shortening
1½ cups sugar

1 cup nuts, chopped
1 tsp. salt
3 cups flour
2 eggs

Cook raisins in water for 20 minutes. Cover with cold water and let stand until ready to use. Mix remaining ingredients, except nuts. Drain all but 1 cup of water off raisins—add raisins and water to the mixture. Add chopped nuts. Spread on cookie sheet. Bake 20-25 minutes in a 325 degree oven. Frost with Penuche Nut Frosting.

PENUCHE NUT FROSTING

1 cup brown sugar, firmly packed   ¼ tsp. salt
¼ cup milk   1 tsp. vanilla
¼ cup shortening   1 cup nuts, chopped

Place brown sugar, milk, shortening and salt in a saucepan. Bring slowly to a full rolling boil, stirring constantly and boil for 1 minute. Remove, beat until lukewarm. Add vanilla, beat until thick enough to spread. The mixture may still be warm. If frosting becomes too thick, add a little cream. Add nuts and spread on cake. Frosts an 8x8x2 inch cake.

KEDRON VALLEY INN
South Woodstock, Vermont

Paul and Barbara Kendall have the spirit of the new Vermont. In their picturesque red brick inn at the bend of the Kedron brook, they have combined the best of bye-gone days with some modern notions of good innkeeping. Paul was born just across the tree-shaded road and is the 7th generation of Kendalls in South Woodstock. It is delightful to hear the brook outside my window, when I'm tucked under the counter-pane in my favorite corner room.

SPICE SQUARES WITH LEMON SAUCE

1 cup sugar   3 cups flour
½ cup butter   1 tsp. soda
3 eggs   ½ tsp. cinnamon
½ cup molasses   ½ tsp. cloves
1 cup chopped raisins   ½ tsp. nutmeg
1 tbsp. milk   dash of allspice

Cream butter and sugar, add eggs well beaten, then molasses. Sift flour soda and spices three times, add to above with milk, add raisins last. Spread thin on baking sheet (18 x 12) and sprinkle with 1 cup chopped walnut meats. Bake in 350 degree oven until brown and gentle touch of fingers leaves no print on cake. Take from oven and cool 10 minutes, cut into 24 - 3'' squares. Serve with clear lemon sauce which is slightly warm. (These keep beautifully in tightly covered tin.)

CLEAR LEMON SAUCE:
4 tbsp. corn starch
1¼ cups sugar
1 cup water
2 tbsp. butter
1 tbsp. grated lemon rind
⅓ cup lemon juice

In heavy saucepan combine water, sugar and cornstarch. Cook stirring constantly until mixture is clear and glossy. Take from heat and add lemon juice, grated lemon rind and butter. Return to heat and bring to boil. Take from heat and keep warm for serving over hot water.

NEW ENGLAND INN
Intervale, New Hampshire

Most of the guest rooms at the New England Inn are in neat little colonial duplex cottages scattered through the pine trees. We found it a very cozy arrangement. I can assure you that I didn't miss any meals—not with offerings like Frozen Lemon Pie, which chef Sam Allen has kindly contributed to this book.

FROZEN LEMON PIE

CRUST:	FILLING:
1 cup of crushed corn flakes	3 eggs separated
⅓ cup butter (melted)	½ cup sugar
3 tablespoons sugar	⅓ cup lemon juice
Mix above ingredients and press firmly into one 9'' pie plate.	1 tablespoon lemon rind
	1 cup heavy cream (whipped)

Beat egg yolks with ¼ cup of the sugar until thickened and lemon colored. Add lemon juice and rind. Beat egg whites until stiff, adding remaining ¼ cup of sugar gradually. Fold egg whites into egg yolk mixture. Whip cream adding 2 drops of lemon food coloring and fold into above mixture. Pour into chilled pie shell and freeze 6 to 8 hours before serving. Garnish with whipped cream and a cherry. This pie is guaranteed to melt the heart of confirmed bachelors and has even made believers out of mothers-in-law.

LAKEVIEW LODGE
Roanoke, Virginia

Spring starts almost after Christmas at the lower end of the Shenandoah Valley in Roanoke, and the travelers enjoy some of the earliest golf of the season at this former horse farm. This Buttermilk Pie is served at its two restaurants.

BUTTERMILK PIE

3 eggs
2¼ cups sugar
4½ tbsp. flour
1½ pts. buttermilk

¾ cup butter
lemon juice
9'' unbaked pastry shell

Beat eggs. Blend in sugar and flour, then add buttermilk and butter. Season to taste with lemon juice. Pour into pastry shell and bake.

STAFFORD'S-IN-THE-FIELD
Chocorua, New Hampshire

Although this inn is tucked away in the New Hampshire woods, there are quite a few rather exotic dishes on the menu. This is because Ramona Stafford is constantly drawing on her experience, particularly her years in California, to create new and tasty recipes. This heavenly pie below is a typical example.

HEAVENLY PIE

SHELL
4 egg whites
¼ tsp. salt

¼ tsp. cream of tartar
1 cup sugar
½ tsp. vanilla

PIE FILLING (enough for two pies)
6 squares semi-sweet chocolate
1 tbs. water
6 tbs. sugar
butter the size of a walnut

1 tbs. heavy cream
3 eggs, plus 1 white
1½ cups heavy cream
3 tbs. powdered sugar

SHELL: Butter a 10-inch pie plate, set oven at 225 degrees. Beat egg whites, salt and cream of tartar until stiff. Beat sugar in gradually and add vanilla. Spread in pie plate making the edges high. Bake about 40 minutes or until dry and firm to the touch. Cool.
FILLING: Melt chocolate in double boiler with 1 tablespoon water. When melted completely, add sugar and stir. Add butter, stir until melted. Remove from heat, add cream. Cool slightly before adding egg yolks one at a time, stirring constantly. Beat egg whites with a pinch of salt to a stiff froth. Pour chocolate over egg whites and fold in carefully. Set aside, keep at room temperature until ready to assemble pie. When pie shell is cool, whip cream with powdered sugar. Spread about 1/3 of whipped cream in bottom of pie shell. Pour in filling, spread remainder of whipped cream on top. Decorate with grated chocolate. Pie should set at least 6 hours. Serves 10.

GREEN MOUNTAIN INN
Stowe, Vermont

Stowe swings in the winter—and in summer, dances a gay waltz. Skiers take over in snow time, and in summer its cool, green mountains beckon us for gentler diversions. Through all seasons the Green Mountain Inn keeps faithful time, and I feel as welcome with my skis, as I do with my golf clubs and tennis racket.

MAPLE CHIFFON PIE

1 envelope unflavored gelatin	2 eggs
2 tbs. cold water	¾ cup heavy cream
2 cups milk	1 tsp. vanilla
2 cups pure maple syrup	¼ to ½ cup broken nut meats
dash of salt	1 nine inch baked pastry shell

Soften gelatin in cold water. Scald milk, maple syrup, and salt in a double boiler. Beat the egg yolks and add syrup mixture gradually while stirring. Return to double boiler and cook over simmering water stirring constantly, until thickened. Remove from heat, add softened gelatin. Stir until dissolved. Cool. Whip cream, add vanilla, and fold into maple custard. Beat egg whites and fold into mixture. Fold in nut meats. Put into pastry shell and chill until firm. Garnish with additional whipped cream.

The key ingredient is the maple syrup. Don't try to get by with sassy substitutes. This disappears in one meal.

MOSELEM SPRINGS INN
Moselem Springs, Pennsylvania

Moselem Springs (pronounced Mosel-em) is an exuberant combination of early Americana and Pennsylvania Dutch. Its history is deep in the roots of eastern Pennsylvania and much care has been taken to preserve an air of antiquity..

MOLASSES COCONUT PIE

½ cup butter	1 cup molasses
¾ cup sugar	1 cup long cut coconut
6 fresh eggs	½ cup water
	2 pinches salt

Turn oven on to 375 degrees. Make 10 inch pie shell. Mix all ingredients together and pour into pie shell. Bake in oven 45 to 50 minutes. This recipe comes from a Pennsylvania Dutch recipe book of the early 1800's and is still a big success with them at Moselem Springs.

KIMBERTON COUNTRY HOUSE
Kimberton, Pennsylvania

The Kimberton Country House is located at a quaint country crossroads with other Pennsylvania stone buildings that have been carefully restored. It is just 45 minutes from downtown Philadelphia through historic Valley Forge Park.

PECAN PIE

4 eggs	1 tsp. vanilla
½ cup sugar	½ cup melted butter
1 cup corn syrup	Pecans

Beat eggs and add sugar. Continue beating with a hand beater as each ingredient is added. Line bottom of 9'' uncooked pie shell with the pecans and pour in the batter. Bake in 350 degree oven for 45 minutes.

Many people dining at Kimberton request this Pecan Pie recipe. After my first piece I could readily understand why. Everybody in my family is an amateur cook. We have taken a crack at making this Pecan Pie, and I must say that it is simple enough to defy even my clumsy efforts. It has one fault; it disappears too fast.

THE GOLDEN LAMB
Lebanon, Ohio

Ohio's oldest inn built in 1805. Noted today for both a rare collection of Shaker tools and artifacts, and a menu that reads like a visit to grandmother's farm. Lodging rooms in this mid-western landmark are named for famous guests of the past. For my visits I've stayed in the Charles Dickens room.

SHAKER SUGAR PIE

½ stick or ⅛ lb. butter
1 cup brown sugar
2 cups light cream
1/3 cup flour

1 tsp. vanilla
nutmeg
9'' unbaked pie shell

Thoroughly mix the flour and brown sugar and spread evenly in the bottom of the unbaked pie shell.
Add the cream and vanilla.
Slice the stick of butter into 12 or 16 pieces and distribute evenly over top of pie. Sprinkle with nutmeg. Bake in 350 degree oven for 40 to 45 minutes or until firm.

BETHEL INN
Bethel, Maine

Bethel is inland Maine, up in the mountains where all the great rivers rise and where the color is so magnificent in spring and fall. The Bethel Inn is one of the remaining old American Plan inns, it even has its own golf course.

BLUEBERRY FRITTERS

1 lb. flour
1 oz. baking powder
1 tsp. salt
2 tbs. sugar

4 eggs, well beaten
2 cups milk
2 tbs. melted shortening
1 pint fresh blueberries

Combine all of the ingredients except the blueberries and blend well to form a batter. Fold in the blueberries. Drop by teaspoon into 360 degree fat.

JORDAN POND HOUSE
Seal Harbor, Maine

Summer afternoon tea on the lawn of the Jordan Pond House is a remarkably soothing experience. The fresh waters of the Jordan Pond ripple against the background of the picturesque low mountains called the Bubbles, and the sun picks up all those resplendent Maine colors.

FRESH PEACH ICE CREAM

1 qt. freshly ground peach pulp with juice (approx. 3 lbs. ripe, whole peaches)
2 to 3 cups granulated white sugar (exact amounts of sugar and lemon juice will depend upon acidity of peaches)
1 qt. heavy cream
1/4 tsp. salt
2 tbsp. fresh lemon juice

Peel and pit fresh ripe juicy peaches; grind, using medium blade. Add sugar, lemon juice and salt; allow to stand approx. 15 minutes; stir occasionally; add heavy cream; mix well. Freeze according to basic deep freeze or electric or hand freezer directions. Yield, approximately 3 qts.
To me, the most fun about making fresh peach ice cream would be in finding a freckled face farm lass to help out. I remember we used to make it this way when I was a boy, and the girl next door used to sit and make faces at me while I churned it by hand. Nothing tastes better than ice cream that you've churned yourself.

THREE VILLAGE INN
Stony Brook, New York

Melons in rum lime sauce . . . the thought of it makes me wish I was sitting at the Three Village Inn right now eating some out of one of their elegant glass dessert dishes.

MELON IN RUM-LIME SAUCE

1 cantaloupe	2/3 cup sugar
1 small honeydew melon	1/3 cup water
1/8 small watermelon	1 tsp. grated lime rind
1 cup fresh blueberries	6 tbs. lime juice
	1/2 cup light rum

Cut the cantaloupe and honeydew melon in half and remove the seeds. Use a melon scoop to form the fruit into small balls. Do the same with the watermelon, working around the seeds. Pile the melon balls and blueberries into a serving bowl and chill.

In a small saucepan mix the sugar with water, bring to a boil and simmer for five minutes. Add the lime rind and allow to cool at room temperature. Stir in the lime juice and light rum. Pour the sauce over the fruit and chill, covered, for several hours. Decorate with sprigs of mint.

Saucy Things

JACK'S CHUTNEY
   Bromley House; Peru, Vermont
BORDELAISE SAUCE
   Bull's Head Inn; Cobleskill, New York
MOLLY PITCHER CRANBERRY RELISH
   Cranbury Inn; Cranbury, New Jersey
HOT FRUIT COMPOTE
   The Pump House Inn; Canadensis, Pennsylvania
KIDNEY BEAN RELISH
   The White Hart Inn; Salisbury, Connecticut
NANA'S CHOCOLATE SAUCE
   Springside Inn; Auburn, New York
STRAWBERRY SUNSHINE
   Doe Run Inn; Brandenburg, Kentucky
SYLLABUB (Holiday Drink)
   Nu-Wray Inn; Burnsville, North Carolina
MARSHLAND'S RHUBARB PUNCH
   Marshland's Inn; Sackville, New Brunswick

BROMLEY HOUSE
Peru, Vermont

This is it—a remote mountain inn with slightly canted floors, country antiques, hooked rugs, fireplaces in the bedrooms, home-made bread, hearty food, good books and records, all with excellent company. I'm looking for old flat irons for the Bromley House collection.

JACK'S CHUTNEY

2 lbs. tart apples
4 cups vinegar
2 lbs. white sugar
1 clove garlic
2 tbs. salt

2 tsp. cayenne pepper
1 pkg. seedless raisins
1 cup currants
8 oz. dates

Peel and chop apples coarsely. Cook in vinegar until transparent. Drain and put in crock. To the remaining vinegar add sugar, garlic, pepper, raisins, currants and dates. Cook in vinegar 10—15 minutes. Pour over apples in crock and cover. Let stand 24 hours. Heat again and put in jars. Don't plan on having this around for very long because it's too good to last.

BULL'S HEAD INN
Cobleskill, New York

When the Bull's Head comes to my mind, I immediately think of beef...whether it be Strip Sir-loin, Roast Beef, or sliced Beef Tenderloin. All of these are from the fires of that open hearth that fill the inn with a delicious aroma. Cobleskill is a real country town a few pleasant miles from the New York State Thruway. The entire region is rich in history.

BORDELAISE SAUCE

4 tbs. butter	1 tsp. salt
4 tbs. minced celery	1 tsp. accent
4 tbs. minced carrots	1 tsp. whole thyme
4 minced shallots	¾ tsp. rosemary leaves
3 tbs. minced parsely	(fresh if possible)
¾ cup dry red wine	½ tsp. crushed corriander seed
2¼ cups rich beef stock	1 tsp. black pepper

¾ cup sliced sauteed fresh mushrooms

Melt butter, saute celery, carrots, shallots and parsley 5 minutes. Add the wine and simmer until reduced one half. Add the remaining ingredients and simmer 15 minutes. Thicken slightly, if desired. Keeps 4 or 5 days in refrigerator. This great sauce is one of the best reasons I know of to have beef twice in the same week. As a leftover, it will add new life to many mundane dishes.

CRANBURY INN
Cranbury, New Jersey

I imagine that the Cranbury Inn, which began life in 1730 as a post house, probably served both Hessians and Patriots in its low ceiling public rooms, before the battle of Monmouth in 1778. Today, among other accomplishments, it contains a truly impressive collection of antique guns and pistols.

MOLLY PITCHER CRANBERRY RELISH

1 qt. cranberries	1 whole orange
2 cups sugar	

Grind 4 cups cranberries. Remove the seeds, then grind one whole orange. Stir the cranberries into the orange and add 2 cups of sugar. Put in covered jars and refrigerate for two (2) days. It is now ready to be used with meat or fowl, or on freshly baked bread.

This little red berry was called ''craneberry'' by early settlers because they grew wild in swamps inhabited by the blue heron. The variations in color are because of different varieties, rather than degrees of ripeness.

THE PUMP HOUSE INN
Canadensis, Pennsylvania

The first time I ever visited the Pump House I enjoyed this most unusual hot fruit compote. The inn is located high in the Poconos, and the dining room has its own waterfall! There are two generations of the Drucquer family involved in keeping this inn, and the third generation is showing a lot of early interest.

HOT FRUIT COMPOTE

½ cup dried prunes, stewed
½ cup peaches, cooked
½ cup pears, cooked
½ cup apricots, cooked
1½ cups fresh applesauce

　juice of ½ lemon & its rind, chopped
1 tsp. cinnamon
½ tsp. ginger
½ tsp. nutmeg

Combine fruit and seasonings and mix well. Bake in covered casserole in 250 degree oven for at least one hour. The longer it bakes the better. A great accompaniment to fish, fowl or meat.

THE WHITE HART INN
Salisbury, Connecticut

The northwest corner of Connecticut is like a Currier and Ives print, with hedgerows, lilac bushes, stone walls and old colonials. The White Hart Inn is right in character. It's over one hundred years old and is an integral part of this independently-minded community. I have browsed for hours among the tantalizing scents of the Country Store which is part of the inn.

KIDNEY BEAN RELISH

1 small onion	1 tbsp. mayonnaise
1 or 2 hard boiled eggs	2 tsp. dill relish
2 cups kidney beans, drained	1 tsp. curry powder
¼ tsp. white pepper	½ tsp. salt
3 stalks celery	

Chop onion, celery and eggs together. Then add beans and mix in mayonnaise, relish and other seasonings. Serve cool and keep under refrigeration. Makes 6 portions.

This is a real New England farm dish and it looks to me as if you could substitute or add wax beans and green beans. Our colonial ancestors got a good deal of mileage from their vegetable gardens.

SPRINGSIDE INN
Auburn, New York

Auburn is in the heartland of central New York State just a few miles south of the thruway. The Springside Inn is at the northern end of Owasco, one of the Finger Lakes. The Spring side is well known for its popovers, Dinner Theatre and the chocolate sauce which is detailed below.

NANA'S CHOCOLATE SAUCE

2¼ cups cocoa
1⅞ cups sugar
¾ cup warm water
¾ oz. vanilla
¼ tsp. salt
 1 oz. dry French Sherry wine

Boil ingredients 3 minutes and remove from heat. When cool beat in Sherry wine.

This chocolate sauce, a suitable topping for ice cream or nut-filled brownies, was given to the innkeeper by his mother-in-law.

Yields 1 quart.

DOE RUN INN
Brandenburg, Kentucky

Four-foot thick limestone walls, large fireplaces and a swift-running stream give the Doe Run a feeling that Daniel Boone has just left it to go hunting in the adjacent forests. The food is Kentucky, served in heaping portions. Although the recipe below is simple, its results are delicious.

STRAWBERRY SUNSHINE

2 cups fresh strawberries, crushed
(Use coarse blade on food grinder)
4 cups sugar
red food coloring (optional)

Mix berries and sugar. Bring to a boil and boil 1 minute. Skim off light foam. Cool. When cool, mix well and pour into sterile jars and seal.

NU WRAY INN
Burnsville, North Carolina

The Nu Wray Inn is famous for the bell that is rung at 8 am every morning to get guests up in time for breakfast which is served promptly at 8:30. As Rush Wray says, "that's the way we do things in Burnsville, North Carolina."

SYLLABUB
(Holiday Drink)

1 qt. cream (24 hours old)   ½ cup grape juice
1 cup fresh milk   ¼ cup orange juice
1 cup sugar   ¼ cup sherry wine
1 tsp. vanilla

Have all of the ingredients cold and place in a large bowl. Beat until frothy. Serve immediately.

MARSHLANDS INN
Sackville, New Brunswick

I love rhubarb, and when I first tasted this delightful concoction at the Marshlands Inn I could hardly believe my taste buds. I can however believe the dozens of postcards I received from guests who recommend both the food and the atmosphere at this seemingly-far-away New Brunswick Inn.

MARSHLANDS RHUBARB PUNCH

Fresh rhubarb, cut in 6'' pieces
6 quarts. water

1 cup granulated sugar
    (per cup of rhubarb juice)
2 parts club soda
    (per 1 part rhubarb syrup)

Fill a 12 quart preserving kettle three-quarters full with fresh rhubarb and add water. Bring to a boil, and boil slowly until the rhubarb is very soft. Strain through a large colander lined with cheesecloth. Measure juice and add 1 cup of sugar per cup of juice. Bring to a boil stirring until all the sugar is dissolved. Boil slowly to a thick syrup. Use a candy thermometer to keep the syrup well under the jelly stage. When thick, pour the syrup into sterilized quart jars and store in a cool place until ready to use.

To serve, add 1 part syrup to 2 parts club soda and stir gently. A few drops of red food coloring may be added if the rhubarb does not have much color.

Index

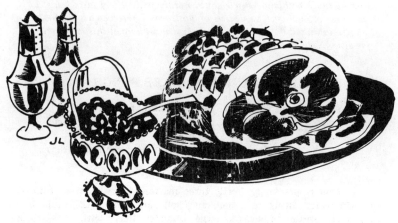